Epworth (

Gener
Harold F. Guit

The Epistle

Epworth Commentaries

The Epistle to the
HEBREWS

PAUL ELLINGWORTH

EPWORTH PRESS

British Library Cataloguing in Publication Data

Ellingworth, Paul
 The Epistle to the Hebrews.
 1. Christinity. Scriptures. Bible. N. T. Hebrews
 I. Title
 227.8707

 ISBN 0–7162–0474–6

First published 1991
by Epworth Press
1 Central Buildings Westminster
London SW1H 9NR

Photypeset by Input Typesetting Ltd, London
and printed in Great Britain by
Billing & Sons Ltd, Worcester

CONTENTS

GENERAL INTRODUCTION

The *Epworth Preacher's Commentaries* that Greville P. Lewis edited so successfully in the 1950s and 1960s having now served their turn, the Epworth Press has commissioned a team of distinguished academics who are also preachers and teachers to create a new series of commentaries that will serve the 1990s and beyond. We have seized the opportunity offered by the publication in 1989 of the Revised English Bible to use this very readable and scholarly version as the basis of our commentaries, and we are grateful to the Oxford and Cambridge University Presses for the requisite licence and for granting our authors pre-publication access. They will nevertheless be free to cite and discuss other translations wherever they think that these will illuminate the original text.

Just as the books that make up the Bible differ in their provenance and purpose, so our authors will necessarily differ in the structure and bearing of their commentaries. But they will all strive to get as close as possible to the intention of the original writers, expounding their texts in the light of the place, time, circumstances, and culture that gave them birth, and showing why each work was received by Jews and Christians into their respective Canons of Holy Scripture. They will seek to make full use of the dramatic advance in biblical scholarship world-wide but at the same time to explain technical terms in the language of the common reader, and to suggest ways in which Scripture can help towards the living of a Christian life today. They will endeavour to produce commentaries that can be used with confidence in ecumenical, multiracial, and multifaith situations, and not by scholars only but by preachers, teachers, students, church members, and anyone who wants to improve his or her understanding of the Bible.

Harold F. Guite
Ivor H. Jones

INTRODUCTION

A congregation consisting largely of university students burst into spontaneous laughter during a reading from Hebrews at the point where, after a somewhat rigorous analysis of the significance of Melchizedek, the writer begins a new paragraph with the disarming words: 'What makes this still clearer . . .' (7.15).

Different parts of the Bible tend, sometimes unfairly, to attract stereotyped images to themselves: Jeremiah is gloomy; the Sermon on the Mount is the simple essence of Christianity; Romans is heavy-going theology; no sane person can understand Revelation; and Hebrews really belongs in the Old Testament. There are of course difficulties in Hebrews, as in any book of the Bible, or any other ancient writing. Yet there is no reason to think that the difficulties are on a different scale from those we meet, for example, in reading Paul's letters.

The difficulties in Hebrews are of two main kinds: broadly speaking, those to do with the outside and the inside of the book.

The problems with the outside of Hebrews may be illustrated by a contrast with Philippians. Although there are problems with the outside of Philippians too (many scholars think it is made up of parts of two or three letters), it is widely agreed that Philippians is a letter written by Paul to Christians in Philippi round about 55 CE, while Paul was in prison, probably in Ephesus.

There is no such agreement about Hebrews. Despite countless theories, Origen (185–253) probably said the last word when he answered the question 'Who wrote Hebrews?' by saying simply 'God knows.' It is probable, despite suggestions to the contrary, that the writer was a man: he uses a masculine form in 11.32 in speaking of himself. It is virtually certain that the author was not Paul, though Hebrews was for long attributed to Paul as a means of claiming for this anonymous writing apostolic authority and a place in the Christian canon. The Greek is smoother than Paul's, and certain key terms, such as 'faith', are used in different though not contradictory ways. Other suggestions have included Luke, Clement of Rome, and even Jude, and Mary, the mother of Jesus. The favourite among modern candidates is Apollos, a suggestion first popularized by Martin Luther; but since we have no other writing by Apollos with which to compare Hebrews, this remains speculation.

Nor do we know where the writer was when he wrote the letter, or where he sent it when he had finished. Scholars are persistently divided about whether Hebrews was written before or after the fall of Jerusalem and the destruction of the Temple in 70 CE.

To say that we do not know the answers to these questions does not mean that we have no evidence at all about the background to Hebrews. Most of the clues are to be found in Hebrews itself. The firmest piece of outside evidence is that Hebrews is clearly referred to by Clement of Rome in his only authentic letter, known as I Clement, written around 96 CE. Otherwise, the strongest piece of evidence about the date of Hebrews is the negative fact that nowhere, in the course of a long argument that God's old covenant with his people 'will shortly disappear' (8.13), does the writer say quietly: 'Indeed, it has disappeared: look at the ruins of the Temple.' News of such a catastrophe must have travelled in a few months to any centre where there was a synagogue. But in fact, the writer shows no interest in what was or was not going on in Jerusalem at the time he wrote: what he says about Jewish worship is based essentially on the Old Testament.

This suggests, though it does not prove, that Hebrews was written some considerable distance from Jerusalem. The writer's way of thinking and writing has been compared with that of Alexandrian writers such as Philo; but the similarities are not close, and it was in Alexandria that Hebrews was first wrongly attributed to Paul. The mention of 'our Italian friends' (13.14) may suggest that Hebrews was written in or near Italy, or alternatively *to* Rome from a place where a number of Italian expatriates were living. Yet Rome was the place where Nero was said to have made Christians the scapegoat for a fire in 64 CE, whereas the writer of Hebrews tells his readers that they 'have not yet resisted to the point of shedding their blood' (12.4). We really do not know. Even the title 'To the Hebrews' is not part of the original text; and even if it were, it would tell us nothing about where those 'Hebrews' lived.

What sort of a writing is Hebrews? There is nothing else quite like it in the New Testament or anywhere else. It is very carefully written, in what is widely considered the best Greek in the New Testament. Yet it is far from a literary exercise: it is written to real people whom the writer knew, even if we do not. Some have thought it to be either one long sermon, taking about an hour to read aloud, or an edited collection of sermons, one of which might have been 3.7–4.13, about God's 'place of rest', and another the famous chapter 11 about the Old Testament heroes of faith. Others have speculated that Hebrews contained early Christian hymns, perhaps in 1.1–4 or 7.1–3; yet although such passages move with a fine free rhythm, there is nothing in them that such a skilled writer could not have written by himself.

It is indeed puzzling that Hebrews ends like a letter but does not begin like one. (I John, which is also called a letter, neither begins nor ends like one, and reads more like a sermon or meditation.) There are two main explanations. The first is that the letter-like ending was added after the rest of Hebrews had been collected: possibly as a covering note to go to another church with the edited collection of sermons. Yet there is no obvious break between the body of Hebrews and its ending; and it is difficult to believe that Hebrews was not written with the special needs of a particular community in mind.

The other main explanation is that Hebrews is a letter from which the opening greetings have been lost. There is no manuscript evidence of this, and certainly no roughness about the stately opening sentence. But it was common practice to provide documents with a protocol or 'glued-on descriptive first leaf' (*Chambers' English Dictionary*). Such a leaf could have become detached from the scroll at an early date, either accidentally or when a copy was sent on to another group. The second explanation covers the facts, but we cannot be sure. In any case, Hebrews is not an abstract treatise but an 'appeal' (13.22; literally, a 'word of encouragement') addressed to real people from whom the writer hoped to be only temporarily separated (13.19). We shall therefore call it a 'letter', as REB and most modern translations do. But it is neither a casual, everyday letter, nor a formal business letter; it is a well planned and persuasively argued piece of writing by someone who believes that some at least of his readers are in grave spiritual danger. He rises to great heights in his concern to meet their need.

At this point we come to the 'inside' problems in understanding Hebrews; problems which concern, not the circumstances in which Hebrews was written, but its content. The author's thought is dominated by two things: the Old Testament, and Christ. There are other possible influences, such as the Dead Sea Scrolls, the writings of the Jewish philosopher Philo (born about 20 BCE, died 50 CE), and trends which later developed into gnosticism; but these are so much less important than the Old Testament that they will be mentioned only in comments on particular verses.

The relation between the two dominant influences is complex. (1) The Old Testament points ahead to Christ; the same God is at work under both the old and the new order or 'covenant'. (2) It is largely with the help of Old Testament texts that the writer explores the significance of Christ, and finds there names which, at least when taken together, are not unworthy of him.

What language shall I borrow
To praise thee, dearest friend?[1]

This is a question all the New Testament writers try to answer in different ways. (3) The author of Hebrews is steeped in the language of the Septuagint or Greek Old Testament; there is no convincing evidence that he knew any Hebrew. This influence goes far beyond the 35 direct quotations of the Old Testament in Hebrews. (4) The Old Testament is a rich mine from which the author draws examples for his readers: both good examples for them to follow (see ch.11), and warnings of what to avoid (see 3.7–4.11). (5) Perhaps most importantly, the coming of Christ shows that, although the Old Testament remains the word of God and of the Holy Spirit (see 3.7; 4. 12–13), the Old Testament itself testifies that what is happening now makes the old order, with its system of priesthood and sacrifice, 'obsolete' (8.13).

All this means that Hebrews cannot be understood on its own: it must be understood as part of the Bible, including the Old Testament. The author of Hebrews would not have put it like that: his Bible *was* the Old Testament. The title 'Old Testament' comes from the Latin equivalent of the Greek for 'old covenant'; but when the writer to the Hebrews speaks of the old covenant, he is referring, not to a book, but to one aspect of its contents.

So how should the modern reader approach Hebrews? 'The modern reader' is an abstraction: the answer to the question of how the reader should approach Hebrews depends on who he or she is. Most people who read Hebrews know more about the rest of the New Testament than they do about the Old. They are often Christians, sometimes new Christians, who find the New Testament hard enough going, and may find Hebrews doubly difficult until they have learned something about its Old Testament background.

More important even than the question of *understanding* Hebrews

---

[1] Paul Gerhardt. 'O sacred Head, sore wounded', *Hymns and Psalms* 176.

through the Old Testament is the question of whether a modern, non-Jewish reader needs to *accept* all the presuppositions on the basis of which Hebrews is written. Presuppositions, assumptions we make before we say anything, are sometimes more important than what we actually say. For example, a modern reader who approaches the gospels on the assumption that miracles don't happen nowadays is likely to understand them differently from the first readers.

So with Hebrews. To take a crucial example, the author seems to say, at one point in his argument, that 'without the shedding of blood there is no forgiveness' (9.22). It is true that this verse refers to the situation 'under the [Old Testament] law'; but the other and more important side of the argument is that, under the new covenant also, there is no forgiveness apart from the shedding of Christ's blood (see ch. 10, especially v. 29). In other words, the writer of Hebrews starts from the presupposition, almost certainly shared by his readers, that there was an essential connection between sacrifice offered to God on the one hand and God's forgiveness of sins on the other. This, for the author and his readers, is what in logic is called an axiom: something which goes without saying and does not need to be discussed. This particular axiom was very widely accepted among both Jews and pagans in the ancient world, and is still accepted by many peoples today. But for many Western readers, the whole system of animal sacrifice, together with its underlying rationale, is at best unreasonable and at worst repulsive. Such readers may well believe that they owe their liberation from sin and their ultimate well-being to Christ, and especially to his self-giving in death; but they may come to that conclusion by a quite different route from the writer to the Hebrews. Those who read Hebrews in a non-Western cultural setting, and have no difficulty with the idea of sacrifice in itself, may nevertheless wish to place their own pre-Christian traditions beside the Old Testament as a possible path to Christ, and thus as a way into the understanding of Hebrews.

The purpose of this brief commentary is twofold: first, to explain what the Letter to the Hebrews meant in its own time; and second, to help present-day readers explore what Hebrews may mean for them, in their very different situations. In the end each reader must complete the second part of the task for himself, for each person's situation is unique, and changes through a human lifetime. But this commentary is written in the conviction that although Hebrews was primarily addressed to Jewish Christians, it is ultimately concerned with the fundamental human condition; indeed, as the writer states from the outset, with 'the universe' (1.2f.). The differences between cultures run deep. But in the end we share the same humanity as the writer of Hebrews and his first readers; and that must make Hebrews ultimately understandable today.

This commentary, like others in this series, is intended for a fairly wide readership. Technical terms are therefore kept to a minimum. The 'synoptic' gospels are Matthew, Mark, and Luke, so called because they generally tell the gospel story from the same point of view. References to them are sometimes given to Mark 'and parallel(s)', meaning the corresponding verses in Matthew and/or Luke. The 'Pastorals' are I and II Timothy and Titus. Scholars differ about whether or not they were written by Paul. This commentary sometimes mentions Paul, without prejudice, in referring to these letters, but does not use them as a basis for distinguishing Paul's thought from that of Hebrews. Similarly, this commentary will not discuss whether sayings attributed to Jesus in the gospels were really spoken by him. Such questions, though important in themselves, were not the concern of the writer of Hebrews, and are not the concern of this commentary either.

The writer to the Hebrews regularly quoted from the Old Testament in Greek. The most widely used Greek translation of the Old Testament is called the Septuagint, from the Latin word for 'seventy', because of a tradition that it was made by seventy translators. In fact the Greek Old Testament was developed over a long period of time, and passed through various stages. It is not always certain which form was used by the writer of Hebrews, so this commentary will normally refer in general terms to 'the Greek Old Testament.'

English versions of the Bible used (cited by their initials) are:

> Authorized (or King James) Version 1611
> Revised Standard Version 1952
> New English Bible 1970
> Good News Bible (also known as Today's English Version) 1976
> New International Version 1979
> New Jerusalem Bible 1985
> Revised English Bible 1989
> New Revised Standard Version 1990

Unless otherwise indicated, quotations are from REB. It will be convenient, though not essential, to use this commentary together with REB, if possible with Apocrypha. Some section headings are taken from the United Bible Societies' Greek New Testament and from GNB.

Occasional references to hymns are to the *Methodist Hymn Book* (1933, cited as *MHB*) or to *Hymns and Psalms* (1983, cited as *HP*).

FOR FURTHER READING

The following list, in order of publication, is limited to books in English which can be read without knowledge of Greek.

Hugh Montefiore, *A Commentary on the Epistle to the Hebrews* (Black's New Testament Commentaries). London: A. & C. Black and New York: Harper and Row 1964. ix + 272 pp. Uses some Greek with explanations.

F. J. Schierse on Hebrews in *The Epistles to the Hebrews, of St James, and to the Thessalonians* (New Testament for Spiritual Reading 9, translated from the German). London: Sheed and Ward 1969. xviii + 123 pp. Based on the author's own translation. Roman Catholic.

George Wesley Buchanan, *To the Hebrews* (The Anchor Bible 36). Garden City, New York: Doubleday 1972. xxx + 271 pp. Based on the author's own translation. More advanced; uses transliterated Hebrew and Greek. Concentrates on Jewish background.

Juliana Casey, I.H.M., *Hebrews* (New Testament Message 18). Wilmington, Delaware: Michael Glazier 1980. xvii + 101 pp. Based on RSV. Roman Catholic.

William G. Johnsson, *Hebrews* (Knox Preaching Guides). Atlanta, Georgia: John Knox Press 1980. 97 pp.

Robert Jewett, *Letter to Pilgrims*. New York: The Pilgrim Press 1981. vi + 248 pp. Based on the author's own translation. The author's theory that Hebrews, like Colossians, was written to Christians in the Lycus Valley has not been generally accepted.

Leon Morris on Hebrews in *Expositor's Bible Commentary*, vol. 12, pp. 1–157. Grand Rapids, Michigan: Zondervan 1981. Based on NIV. Evangelical.

Raymond Brown, *The Message of Hebrews. Christ above All* (The Bible Speaks Today). Leicester, U.K. and Downers Grove, Illinois, Inter-Varsity Press 1982. 272 pp. Based on RSV. Evangelical.

Donald Guthrie, *The Letter to the Hebrews* (Tyndale New Testament Commentaries). Leicester U.K.: Inter-Varsity Press, and Grand Rapids, Michigan: Eerdmans 1983. 281 pp. Evangelical.

Donald A. Hagner, *Hebrews* (A Good News Commentary). San Francisco: Harper & Row 1983. xxviii + 257 p. Based on GNB.

George W. MacRae, S.J., *Hebrews* (Collegeville Bible Commentary 10). Collegeville, Minnesota: The Liturgical Press 1983. 60 pp. Roman Catholic. Based on the New American Bible. Includes questions for discussion.

Robert H. Smith, *Hebrews* (Augsburg Commentary on the New Testament). Minneapolis, Minnesota: Augsburg Publishing House 1984. 207 pp. Recommends RSV. Lutheran.

William L. Lane, *Call to Commitment. Responding to the Message of Hebrews*. Nashville, Tennessee etc.: Thomas Nelson Publishers 1985. 185 pp. Stimulating.

R. McL. Wilson, *Hebrews* (New Century Bible Commentary). Grand Rapids, Michigan: Eerdmans, and Basingstoke, U.K.: Marshall Morgan & Scott 1987. xii + 268 pp. Based on RSV.

Albert Vanhoye, S.J., *Structure and Message of the Epistle to the Hebrews* (Subsidia Biblica 12). Rome: Editrice Pontificio Istituto Biblico 1989. ix + 120 pp. By the Roman Catholic author of many distinguished studies in French, especially on the literary structure of Hebrews. Not a commentary.

F. F. Bruce, *The Epistle to the Hebrews* (New International Commentary on the New Testament). Grand Rapids, Michigan: Eerdmans, revised edition 1990. xxii + 426 pp. Originally published in 1964, this thorough but readable evangelical commentary is now based on the author's own translation; Greek and transliterated Hebrew are used in the footnotes.

A commentary by the present author will be published by Eerdmans in the New International Greek Testament Commentary.

Most of the ancient non-biblical writings mentioned in this commentary may be found in:

The Old Testament Pseudepigrapha, ed. James H. Charlesworth. Garden City, New York: Doubleday, and London: Darton, Longman and Todd. Two volumes, 1983, 1985.

Early Christian Writings: the Apostolic Fathers, translated by Max Staniforth, with introductions and new editorial material by Andrew Louth. Harmondsworth, U.K.: Penguin Books, revised edition 1987.

1.1–4   *God has spoken by his Son*

This impressive prologue forms a single sentence in Greek, as in the Authorized Version: 'God, who at sundry times and in diverse manners spake in times past unto the fathers by the prophets, hath in these last days spoken unto us by his son . . .' In this sentence the writer does four things.

First, he contrasts what happened in Old Testament times with what has happened in Christ. (1) The Old Testament revelation came *in many and varied ways*; as the writer will state repeatedly later on, revelation in Christ is *once for all* (7.27; 9.26–28). (2) The Old Testament revelation came *in times past . . . to our forefathers*; the new revelation has come *in this the final age . . . to us*. (3) The Old Testament revelation came *through the prophets*; the new revelation has come through God's Son.

Second, the writer points out that both the old and the new revelation are part of one unchanging purpose. He recognizes, in effect, that in order for things to be contrasted they must have something in common. Under both the old order and the new, it is one and the same God at work; and whatever *signs and wonders* (2.4) accompany his activity, his revelation is best described by saying that he *spoke* or *has spoken*. This is Hebrews' counterpart to what John 1.1–18 says about God's eternal Word which became a human being.

Third, the writer outlines who Christ is, and what he has done. This is the main point of this prologue, so it is discussed in much greater detail. (1) Christ is God's 'Son'. Literally, God *has spoken to us in* (or 'by') 'a Son'. 'A Son' does not, of course, mean that Jesus is one among many divine sons (though people who follow Jesus are in a wider sense his 'many sons' (2.10)). It means that the one through whom God has now spoken is fitly called 'Son'. (2) God has *appointed* his Son *heir of all things*. This is a way of saying that God has given the universe to his Son, so that it belongs to him by right. When Israel took possession of the promised land, God gave each tribe and family its allotted piece of land. In the same way, God has given everything to his Son (3) This gift is appropriate, because the Son was active from the beginning in creation. *Through him he created the universe*, literally 'through whom he made the worlds', is one of Hebrews' tremendous throw-away lines (for another, see 11.38), in which a

1

great truth is expressed in a subordinate clause. The implication here is that even creation is secondary by comparison with the new thing that God has now done through Christ. (4) The Son is *the radiance of God's glory, the stamp of God's very being*. The language here owes something to what was said about wisdom in the Apocrypha (sometimes known as the deuterocanonical books), Wisd. 7.22–8.1; especially the uncommon word for *radiance*, which REB less happily translates 'effluence' in Wisd. 7.23. The Son is as inseparable from God as a sunbeam from the sun; as perfectly and permanently like him as the image on a coin is like the die which stamps it. (5) What Christ is cannot be separated from what he has done; and the purpose and effect of his work was to purify people from their sins. The writer will later argue in detail that although this was also the purpose of the Old Testament sacrifices, only Christ was able to achieve that purpose in more than an external sense. For the time being, the writer refers to this important matter almost in passing. (6) God has recognized what Christ has done by raising him to his right hand in heaven. This picture language means that Christ is uniquely close to God, and therefore supreme over all other things. Hebrews says little about the resurrection of Jesus, though he believes in it (see 13.20); the word *raised* in v. 4, literally 'having become', does not refer to the resurrection. The exaltation or ascension of Jesus to God's right hand seems more important in the writer's own thinking; he refers to it again and again (see 8.1; 10.12; 12.2), in language drawn from Ps. 110.1, part of which will be quoted in v. 13.

Fourth, what God has done in Christ is greater than anything he did before. In particular, God has given to his Son a position higher than that of the angels. This will be the main theme in the rest of ch. 1, and to some extent also in ch. 2 (see vv. 5,9,16). Some translations, such as GNB, therefore start a new section with 1.4, even though grammatically it is still the same sentence as 1.1–3. Hebrews usually moves smoothly from one point to another, so modern section headings should not be taken too seriously. In any case, in the earliest manuscripts, there are not only no sections and paragraphs, but no divisions between sentences or even words.

That is the general outline of this brief but tightly packed prologue. A few words and phrases need special comment.

1.1   The word for *in times past* probably means 'long ago'; this makes a better contrast with *this the final age*. The writer seems mainly interested in the period from Abraham to the entry into the promised land. He also seems to have been impressed by the sufferings of the

2

Jews under Antiochus Epiphanes in the early 160s BCE (see comment on ch. 11); but there were no prophets at that time.

To our forefathers is literally 'to the fathers'. 'Fathers' often means 'ancestors', as here; women are not excluded (see for example 11.11). Jewish readers of Hebrews would naturally think of the great Old Testament heroes as 'our' forefathers; but the writer may have tactfully avoided saying so, for the sake of any non-Jews who might read his letter.

The prophets are the well-known Old Testament prophets, whose books by this time were considered authoritative, alongside the rest of our Old Testament, namely the Law of Moses and the 'Writings'. The word for 'through' is the same as that translated 'in' in the phrase 'in his Son'. Here it may mean 'in the prophets' writings'.

1.2   *In this the final age* probably means both that God's revelation in the Son is recent, and that it is final: the last age has begun.

The words translated *the universe* sometimes mean 'the ages'; but here the writer is thinking in terms of space rather than time, so 'the universe' here and in *v.3* probably means the same as 'all things'.

1.4   *The angels*, in the Old Testament, are spiritual beings who surround God in heaven as courtiers attend a king. The same picture is found in the Old Testament and in the Dead Sea Scrolls. Beliefs about the angels developed considerably between the Old and New Testament periods. Particular angels are sometimes given special tasks, such as representing a nation, protecting an individual, or delivering messages from God, especially the Law (see 2.2). The writer of Hebrews thinks of them mainly as God's servants, working on behalf of God's people (see 1.14). Some people think that the first readers of Hebrews, like the church at Colossae (see Col. 2.18,23), were in danger of worshipping angels alongside or instead of Christ, but this does not seem to be the main danger which the writer fears for them.

The title, literally 'a name', is the last word in this long Greek sentence; it therefore carries great emphasis. But what is this 'name'? The writer uses the name 'Jesus' sparingly and at key points in the letter (see 2.9); he is not likely to be referring to this name here. 'Lord', perhaps the first title given to Jesus (see Phil. 2.9–11), is not often used in Hebrews outside Old Testament quotations; see 2.3; 13.20, where 'the Lord' refers to Jesus. The rest of ch. 1 suggests that the writer is thinking here of Jesus' status as Son of God, a title already used in v.2. It is possible, however, that he does not specify what 'name' God gave to Jesus when he exalted him, because he is already thinking also of the other great title of Jesus in Hebrews, namely that of high priest, first used in 2.17.

This raises the final question about this introduction to the letter: what effect did the writer intend it to have on the first readers? Like any good teacher, he begins where his readers are, and tries to lead them on to something fresh. In particular, he wishes to build on the already traditional Christian faith, which they seem to be in danger of taking for granted and undervaluing, and thus show them that there is no alternative to Christ. So in this passage he reassures them by reminding them of things they already know and believe, such as the Old Testament revelation, Jesus as Son of God, and his sacrifice and exaltation. But he also points his readers to a deeper understanding of Christ by building up a great picture of all Jesus has done, and by insisting that his *title*, whatever it is, shows that God has given him the highest place in heaven.

1.5–14   *The Son and the angels*

It is fair to assume that angels played a larger part in the thinking of the first readers of Hebrews than they do for most people today. This passage makes the startling claim that Jesus enjoys a higher status than any angel; in other words, that he is closer to God than any other being, even in heaven. What is more, the writer supports this claim by quoting a chain of no less than seven Old Testament texts, thus appealing to an authority which both the writer and his readers must have recognized as being beyond argument or appeal.

The underlying argument runs as follows:

(1) Jesus is the Son of God. This is not new teaching: this title is used throughout the New Testament (for example, Mark 1.1; Matt. 4.3,6; John 20.31; Acts 9.20; Rom. 1.4). The writer of Hebrews appears to assume that his readers already acknowledge Jesus as God's Son. Old Testament texts which refer to a son of God may therefore be applied to Jesus.

(2) Just as a human son is closer to his father than a servant is, so the Son of God has higher status than the angels, who are merely God's servants.

(3) Therefore Jesus has a higher status than the angels.

At the end of the chapter, as the writer prepares to speak about the relationship between Jesus and believers, he draws a corollary or further conclusion from his argument: angels are not only *God's* servants; God appoints angels to serve his people. So in a sense angels are our servants too.

Much of this argument may leave a modern reader cold, for three reasons.

First, a modern reader may not be attracted by the method of arguing from proof texts. There are two answers to this. The first is that the writer of Hebrews (unlike the Qumran writers) rarely if ever quotes Old Testament texts in isolation from their context. It is true that he is not trying to write a complete and systematic commentary on Old Testament passages. In particular he avoids Old Testament references to enemies and to Gentiles, even then they occur close to verses which he does quote. It is also true that his way of understanding Old Testament texts is often not that of a modern scholar; but that is scarcely to be expected. By the standards of his time, however, he uses the Old Testament carefully and responsibly, as we shall see when we examine the quotations one by one. His use of the Old Testament is always founded on what he takes to be the literal meaning of the text. Even his brief note on the origin of the name 'Melchizedek' (7.2) is nothing compared with the free-wheeling, often spiritualizing allegory which we find in different forms in the Jewish philosopher Philo, in the Dead Sea Scrolls, and in later Christian writers such as Origen and Augustine.

The second answer is that the writer of Hebrews is not reading the Old Testament on his own. It is scarcely an exaggeration to say that in New Testament times the entire Christian community was 'studying the scriptures' (Acts 17.11; compare John 5.39) in order to discover adequate answers to the persistent question: 'Who is Jesus?' (compare Mark 4.41 and parallels). Sometimes, Hebrews builds on familiar texts such as Ps. 110.1, which had already been used, probably even by Jesus himself, to point towards an answer to this question; see Mark 12.35ff. and parallels, and the comment on Heb. 1.13. At other times, like Paul and other New Testament writers, he moves out to explore less familiar texts. Yet even when he does this, he does so, not as an isolated individual, but as a member of a community urgently engaged in the same type of creative research. Even what is probably his most original piece of Old Testament interpretation, his application to Jesus of Ps. 110.4 (see note on Heb. 5.6), comes from a psalm already well thumbed in Christians' copies of the psalter. It is of course possible to argue that the entire Christian community was mistaken in trying to find Christ in the Old

Testament. But what else could they do, to what other authority could they turn, if they were not to conclude, like followers of the heretic Marcion (died about 160 CE), that Christ was a bolt from the blue, sent by an otherwise unknown God? What else can we do but attempt to trace God's continuing purpose throughout the whole history of his people?

A second obstacle for a modern reader is that he may not be particularly interested in angels. They are not mentioned in the earliest Christian confessions of faith, nor in the Apostles' or the Nicene Creed; they may therefore be supposed to lie on the edge of Christian belief. To this problem, too, there is a twofold answer. First, although the writer and his readers clearly believe in angels, angels do not play a central part in Hebrews as a whole. After the first two chapters, they are mentioned only in two Old Testament references (11.18; 13.2), and in passing among other inhabitants of the heavenly Jerusalem (12.22). There is nothing like the descriptions of angelic hierarchies which are found in Jewish writings before and after the New Testament; nor is Melchizedek (7.1–10) represented as an angel, as he was at Qumran. Yet the discussion of angels in chapter 1 is indirectly important for the argument as a whole. If Jesus, as Son of God, is more than an ordinary human being, if he is more, even, than just another angel, then there is no one better, indeed no one else, to whom the readers can turn for help in matters of eternal life and death.

The other part of the answer is to question our own tendency to assume that even if angels exist, they do not matter. As Hamlet put it:

> There are more things in heaven and earth, Horatio,
> Than are dreamed of in your philosophy.

Many people in the West are finding that neglect or rejection of Christianity leaves a vacuum which is often filled by belief in occult forces; forces which, though they may not be God, are thought to be more powerful than human beings. To this, Hebrews, in general agreement with the rest of the Bible and Christian tradition, replies that there are indeed such forces, some good, some evil, but that they are all under God's control and subject to Christ.

Third, a modern reader may be impatient with this whole discussion of the status of Christ, and may rightly object that status was the last thing Jesus sought. To this, the writer to the Hebrews responds as follows. (1) It is not a question of what Jesus sought, but of what God has given him (v. 4). (2) The supremacy of Christ is only one side of the coin; the other side is the human Christ who suffered (2.17f.; 4.15). Hebrews contains the germ of what later theologians would call the divine and human 'natures' of Christ, united in a single 'person'. (3) The supremacy of Christ means power for a purpose, and power to be used not for himself but for others: to break evil's hold on humanity once for all (2.14), and thus 'save completely those who approach God through him' (7.25).

Before we turn to the individual quotations, there is one more general matter to note. The practice of quoting Old Testament texts in a series, or 'chain' (*catena*), seems to have been widespread in New Testament times and later. Similar chains have been found among the Dead Sea Scrolls; Rom. 3.10–18 is another New Testament example. Some people have thought that the writer of Hebrews took this chain ready-made from some other source; but there is little overlap between the texts Hebrews quotes here, and other such chains which have survived. On the whole it is best to assume that the writer of Hebrews studied the Old Testament for himself and built up his own collection of quotations, using some texts which are used elsewhere in the New Testament, and other texts which are not. His purpose was to build up a cumulative argument on the basis of the testimony of God in Scripture.

1.5 *To which of the angels . . . ?* The writer does not expect an answer. It is a rhetorical question, like the corresponding question in v. 13; a way of saying emphatically: 'God never said to any angel . . .' The first quotation comes from Ps. 2.7. It corresponds exactly to the Greek Old Testament and to the meaning of the Hebrew words. In the psalm the king is announcing the decree by which God has appointed him to rule over Israel, and 'today' is the day of his coronation. Since the psalm continued to be sung in the Temple, it must have been reapplied to a succession of rulers. Paul quotes it in Acts 13.33, applying it to the resurrection of Jesus. The writer of Hebrews quotes it again in 5.5, understanding it in both places as referring to Jesus' exaltation. He does not comment on the word 'today', and this word is not emphasized; emphasis falls rather on 'you' and 'I', and to some extent on 'Son'. It is therefore not certain whether the writer thinks of 'Son' as a title first given to Jesus at the time of his exaltation, or whether, as is more likely, the title belonged to him eternally.

'*I have become your father*' is literally ' "I have begotten you" '; modern English seems to have no natural equivalent for 'beget'. The language is of course figurative both in the psalm and in Hebrews.

In the psalm it refers to God's recognition or 'adoption' of the king of Israel; in Hebrews to God's recognition of Jesus' unique status.

'*I shall be his father*. . . .': the second quotation comes either from II Sam. 7.14 or from I Chron. 17.13, where the wording is the same. In both places, the prophet Nathan is delivering a message from God to King David, telling him that not he, but his son Solomon, will be allowed by God to build the temple which David had planned. God is therefore saying of Solomon, as he has said of the unnamed king in Ps. 2, that he will adopt him as his son, thereby choosing and recognizing him as king. The writer of Hebrews may have the Chronicles passage in mind, since the parallel passage in II Samuel goes on to mention the possibility of Solomon falling into sin.

In this second quotation, unlike the first, the word 'father' is used in speaking of God. It is a surprising fact that nowhere else in Hebrews is God called 'father' without qualification; in 12.9 he is called 'the father of spirits', which REB translates 'our spiritual Father'. Too much stress should not be laid on this, but it is one of several features which suggest that Hebrews' picture of God is perhaps more severe than that of other New Testament writers.

The modern reader may object that it is dishonest for the writer to take a text which refers to Solomon, and reapply it to Christ. There are various possible answers to this objection. First, it may be said that the writer did not look at the context; but this would be against his normal practice. Second, the Old Testament passage, though referring directly to Solomon, also mentions all David's 'house' or descendants, among whom Jesus was numbered. Third, the writer and his readers probably agreed that Jesus fulfilled perfectly, as Solomon did not, what God said about Solomon through Nathan.

1.6   The introduction to the next quotation raises three related questions. First, does *again* merely introduce another quotation, as in the second part of v. 5; or does it mean 'when he brings again the firstborn . . .'? REB is probably right in choosing the first option.

Second, why does 'the Son' suddenly become *the firstborn*? John speaks of God's 'only' son (1.14,18; 3.16,18), though Paul speaks of believers as God's 'sons' (Rom. 8.14,19; II Cor. 6.18; Gal. 3.26). For Hebrews, the most likely answer is that the writer is already anticipating what he will say in chapter 2 about the relationship between Christ and believers, who are called 'many sons' (2.10: see also 12.23).

Third, what is this *world* to which the *firstborn* is presented? The Greek word is *oikoumené*, 'inhabited world', from which the English word 'ecumenical' is derived. Here, it may mean either this world, to which Jesus might be said to have been *presented* when he was born; or 'the world (*oikoumenē*) to come', as in 2.5, to which Jesus was 'presented' at the time of his exaltation. The latter is much more likely: God is thought of as calling on his heavenly court to welcome one who is greater than them all, and to recognize him as supreme.

It is not quite certain where this quotation comes from. The most likely explanation is that the writer was quoting from some Greek form of Deut. 32.43 which is now lost, but for which a Hebrew text found at Qumran gives some support. Less probably, the quotation is from Ps. 97.7. It is not impossible that the writer of Hebrews had both texts in mind. In any case, he understands God to be the speaker. It is true that the quotation speaks of *God's angels* rather than 'my angels'; but the writer does not make unnecessary changes to his quotations.

1.7–12 The next three quotations are linked: the first, about the angels, is contrasted with the next two, longer, quotations about the Son, with whom the writer is more concerned. In the first of these quotations (v. 7) and the third (vv. 10–12), God is represented as speaking *about* the angels or the Son, while in the second (vv. 8–9) he is speaking *to* the Son; fortunately, the same Greek word has both meanings.

1.7 The quotation comes from Ps. 104.4, which REB translates:

> You make the winds your messengers,
> flames of fire your servants.

In the Greek Old Testament, which the writer of Hebrews probably quotes accurately from his text, the meaning seems to be the other way round, namely that God turns his messengers into winds, and his ministers into flames of fire. What this meant to the writer of Hebrews is uncertain, but the main point is that the angels are 'servants'. In Hebrew poetry, a second line often overlaps considerably in meaning with the first; so in this case, 'angels' = 'ministers'. The word for 'ministers' is related to the word translated *ministering* before *spirits* in v. 14. In v. 7, the point is that the angels are God's servants, whereas in v. 14, they serve believers. *His*, in both lines of the quotation, may mean, not 'God's', but 'Christ's'. The writer has already said that the Son shared in creation (v. 2), and 'sustains the universe' (v. 3).

1.8f.   The quotation is taken from Ps. 45.6f., with some variation from the Greek Old Testament. The first few words may be translated 'God is your throne . . .'. More probably, this is one of the few places in the New Testament, and the only place in Hebrews, where Jesus is directly called 'God'. Most if not all such texts involve worship rather than theological statement, as here (compare John 20.28; perhaps also Rom. 9.5, see REB note).

The grammar of the quotation is difficult: in v. 8, one would expect *your throne* to be followed by 'your kingdom', not *his kingdom*, especially since we have 'you' again in v. 9. REB, probably correctly, follows three Greek manuscripts of the highest quality, against all others which have the less awkward 'your kingdom'. In any case, the whole quotation refers to the Son. A possible expanded translation would run:

But God says *to the Son*:
   'Your throne, O God, is for ever and ever';

and:

   'The sceptre of justice is the *sceptre of his* [the Son's] *kingdom.'*

The psalm itself was probably written to celebrate a king's wedding. REB translates the first line 'God has enthroned you for all eternity', since Israelite kings, unlike those of surrounding nations, were never thought of as divine. It was natural for the psalm to be reinterpreted as pointing to the righteous king who was to come, God's Anointed *par excellence*, the Messiah. The reference in v. 9 to *anointing you with oil* made this development almost inevitable.

1.10–12   The quotation is from Ps. 102.25–27. The introduction, which is simply *and*, implies 'God also says to the Son.' The writer generally follows his Greek Old Testament text, but the Hebrew does not have 'you, Lord', words important for the argument of Hebrews. *You will fold them up*, literally 'you will roll them up', is 'you will cast them off' in the Hebrew; the text of Hebrews, found also in some Greek Old Testament texts, recalls Isa. 34.4:

All the host of heaven will crumble into nothing,
the heavens will be rolled up like a scroll.

The writer of Hebrews takes a text which in the Old Testament refers to God, and applies it to Jesus. 'Jesus is Lord' is the earliest Christian confession of faith (Acts 11.17,20; Rom. 10.9; I Cor. 12.3). The word for 'Lord' could in itself mean no more than 'sir', but it was also the normal Greek equivalent of Yahweh, the Hebrew proper name for God. To call Jesus 'Lord' here is thus not an anticlimax: it reinforces the title 'God' in v. 8. The title 'Lord' is however not much used in Hebrews outside Old Testament quotations; it is used of Jesus in 2.3, and the final blessing (13.20) is in the name of 'our Lord Jesus'. The quotation re-emphasizes what has already been said about Jesus as existing from eternity, and as sharing in the work of creation (1.2). It also points to what the writer says later about Christ as the only fixed point in a universe which will be shaken by God's final judgment (12.27–29), the only one who remains 'the same yesterday, today, and for ever' (13.7). The moral for the readers is clear; they have already come to believe in Jesus as Lord, and this is no time to devalue or abandon that faith.

1.13   The series of quotations ends with part of the most frequently quoted verse in the New Testament: Ps. 110.1. It has already been alluded to, but not directly quoted, in 1.3, in connection with Jesus' sitting at God's right hand. The writer does not quote the first part of the verse, which Jesus had used in controversy with the scribes to show that the Messiah would be more than a descendant of David (Mark 12.35–37 and parallels). It is very likely, however, that the writer knew that other Christians were applying this text to Jesus (see also Mark 14.62 and parallels; 16.19; Acts 2.34–35; Rom. 8.34; I Cor. 15.25; Eph. 1.20; Col. 3.1; Heb. 10.12,13; 12.2). The use of such a familiar text, like the writer's re-telling of Israel's history in chapter 11, must have encouraged his first readers to believe that he wished to strengthen rather than disturb their common faith. No one but Jesus, he repeated – certainly no angel – has been given the supreme place of honour in God's presence.

This interpretation is in line with the way in which the writer has reapplied other Old Testament texts to Jesus. In its Old Testament setting, Ps. 110, like Ps. 2, quoted in Heb. 1.5, showed God speaking to a king of Israel, probably on the day of his enthronement. The psalm had doubtless been reapplied many times to different rulers in the course of Temple worship in Jerusalem. Now the writer of Hebrews, like other Christians, claims it for Christ, as Jesus had implicitly claimed it for himself.

In other respects, the quotation is not in Hebrews' own style. The writer consistently avoids referring to *enemies* of God, Jesus, or the church, except when he quotes this verse again in 10.13. The closest he comes is when he mentions 'those who oppose God' (GNB) in 10.27 (REB translates 'enemies', but the Greek is milder). The writer works by peaceful persuasion rather than by vigorous controversy (as Paul, for example in Gal. 1.6–9; also II Peter and Jude). *Sit at my right hand until I make your enemies your footstool* does not necessarily mean that Jesus is thought of as standing up, or moving from God's right side, once his enemies have been defeated. (A similar use of 'until' is found in Matt. 1.25.) There are ancient statues showing victorious rulers with their feet literally resting on the necks of conquered enemies; but both Ps. 110 and Hebrews use this language figuratively.

1.14   This phase of the argument is rounded off, and a fresh one introduced, with another rhetorical question. It means that angels are all 'spirits who serve God' (GNB). As the quotation in v. 6 has already shown, God has also ordered them to worship his Son; there is no rivalry in heaven. Now the writer makes a further point which will be central throughout chapter 2: God sends them out to help those who are to be saved. REB's *destined* is stronger than the Greek, which simply points to a future event. *Receive* is related to the word translated 'heir' in v. 2: it implies 'receive as God's gift'. The writer will have more to say about *salvation* in 2.1–4; it is the word translated 'deliverance' in 2.3. As always in Hebrews (and in a different way in Paul), the high theological statements about who Jesus is, and what he has done, are related to the writer's concern for what is in danger of happening to his first readers; a golden rule for all Christian teaching and preaching.

2.1–4   *The great salvation*

Some of Paul's letters to churches are divided into two main parts: the first mainly doctrinal, the second a practical appeal to his readers (note for example the change of gear at Rom. 9.1 and Col. 3.1). Hebrews is different: the writer moves repeatedly back and forth between teaching and exhortation. This section contains his first direct appeal to his readers. It is linked with the teaching of ch. 1 by the words: 'that is why . . .' If Jesus holds a higher place than angels in heaven, it is folly to 'ignore' the salvation (or 'deliverance') which he has brought.

In this appeal, as often, the author places himself alongside his readers: *We are bound . . . what we have been told . . . what escape can there be for us if we ignore so great a deliverance?* From one point of view, this is part of the author's strategy of tactful persuasion, such as every preacher uses, and which the author deploys with particular skill. But it is more than that. Later, when his probe approaches more sensitive spots, he addresses his readers as 'you', and even, it seems, has particular individuals in mind ('any one of you', 4.1; compare 12.15–16), though he never names names. It is therefore best to take his use of 'we' seriously; that is, to understand his warnings as including himself (compare I Cor. 9.27). This will help us understand his later, more severe warnings in 6.4–6 and 10.26–31).

This passage is also important because it shows one aspect of the relation between the old order and the new; in other words, between Old Testament religion and Christ. From one point of view, now that Christ has come, the old order is 'becoming obsolete' (8.13) – though the author approaches this statement with extreme care, suggesting that the old ways of worship still meant a great deal to his Jewish readers. From another point of view, however, the Old Testament remains the word of God, a source of authoritative quotations (ch. 1), and also of examples both for encouragement (ch. 11) and for warning (as here; see also the Introduction, p. xii). From the first point of view, the argument follows the pattern: 'Not angels/animal sacrifices/levitical priests . . . but Christ.' From the second point of view, the author uses a 'much more' or 'how much more' argument widely used in the gospels (for example Matt. 6.30, . . . 'will he not all the more clothe you?'; 7.11; 10.25), elsewhere in the New Testament (Rom. 5.10,15,17; 11.12,24), in other Jewish writings, and in other cultures. This type of argument, called *a fortiori* in Latin and *qal waḥomer* in Hebrew, is frequent in Hebrews (for example, 9.14; 10.25; 12.9,25). It points to the writer's belief that God's revelation in Christ, though final and complete, formed part of a purpose which can be traced throughout Israel's history. How and when to use each of these two approaches is a question which one cannot avoid when preaching to people, at home or abroad, whose traditions have points both of similarity and contrast with the Christian faith.

2.1   *That is why*, literally 'because of this', points both backwards to the argument of chapter 1, and forwards to vv. 2–4, which will also explain *what we have been told*, literally 'the (things) heard'. The words *drifting from our course* probably evoke the picture of a ship in a storm, in danger of being swept past the entrance to a harbour.

2.2–4   is a single sentence in Greek, almost as impressive as 1.1–4. Paul shows the same tendency as Hebrews to write long sentences at the opening of letters and in passages of high emotion. The writer of Hebrews generally keeps them under better control than Paul, and thus serves as a better model for modern preachers and writers, who are advised that the full stop is a precious aid to understanding.

2.2 refers, like Acts 7.38,53 and Gal. 3.19, to a Jewish tradition, not found in the Old Testament, that angels served as intermediaries through whom God gave the law to Moses. This tradition is part of a general tendency, in the later centuries before Christ, to emphasize God's distance from human beings. That is not the writer's concern here. The argument rather runs:

> God's law was given *through angels*.
> It had absolute authority.
> In particular, anyone who disobeyed it was punished.
> Jesus has brought salvation.
> He has even higher authority than angels (see ch. 1).
> So there is no hope for anyone who rejects his salvation.

The argument is not in fact quite so neat as this bare outline might suggest. There is contrast as well as comparison between the old order and the new: the keynote of the old order is its *demand* for obedience; the keynote of the new order is its *offer* of salvation. (A preacher who leaves his hearers with a message of demand is therefore still moving in the world of the Old Testament.) Parts of Hebrews, including this passage, are indeed 'demanding'; but Hebrews' most terrible warnings are addressed to those who reject God's final offer in Christ, and the writer intends the letter as a whole as a 'message of encouragement' (13.22).

From the middle of v. 3 to the end of this passage, the writer speaks in greater detail about the 'salvation' or *deliverance* which Christ has brought. He does not attempt a definition; he does not yet even say what exactly it is that Christ has done. Instead, he appeals to the other great source of their Christian conviction: to their Christian experience, which confirms and revitalizes the message of the Old Testament. He calls the readers' attention (1) to the source of that deliverance in *the Lord* Jesus himself, referring at this stage mainly to his teaching; (2) to the reliable *testimony* of those who listened personally to Jesus and brought the message to the community to which Hebrews is written; and (3) to the miraculous activity of the *Holy Spirit* which added the testimony of God himself to what the messengers said. The whole stress is on the overwhelmingly secure basis of the writer's and the readers' faith. Their faith rests, not merely on inward feeling, nor even only on the authority of God's written word, but on a living tradition including words which the readers themselves had heard, and events which they had seen. For many modern readers, this will be a more direct approach than through the Old Testament; but in Hebrews the one complements the other.

This passage tells us a little about the writer and his readers. The author does not claim to have seen and heard Jesus personally, or to be an apostle; indeed, nowhere does he claim any authority for himself, even when (as here) he is claiming supreme authority for the message about Jesus. Many people have thought that this passage, and what is said elsewhere about the readers' declining faith, suggests that the readers were second or third generation Christians. But this is not necessarily so: John Wesley wrote in his *Journal* for 18 June 1739 about the recently founded Methodist society in Bristol: 'It is scarce credible what advantage Satan had gained during my absence of only eight days. Disputes had crept into our little society, so that the love of many was already waxed cold.' It has also been thought that the extraordinary miracles of the early days had ceased, and that this was a reason for the readers' faith growing cold; but the writer does not say so, and does not mention these miracles elsewhere.

In 2.2, the word for *violation* means 'transgression', literally 'over-stepping the mark'; the word for *disobedience* may also mean 'unwillingness to hear' (compare 3.7,15f.; and contrast what will be said of Christ's obedience in 10.5–10; compare also 12.3–11). The word translated *penalty* can also mean 'reward' (as in 10.35, 11.26, but clearly not here); in philosophical ethics, the noun 'sanction' may also have a positive or a negative meaning.

2.3 *Ignore*, like 'drifting' in v. 1, suggests that the danger which the writer fears for his readers is not that of deliberately setting out on some evil course, or enthusiastically adopting some wrong belief, but rather passively letting go of their faith in Christ; he later uses the word 'lax' (6.12). Yet this laxity, this lack of 'resolution' (12.1) may in the end amount to the ultimate sin of deliberate (10.26) rejection of Christ.

2.4 *Gifts . . . distributed* is literally 'divisions' (compare 4.12). The language is different from Paul's in I Cor. 12, but the thought is similar. Otherwise, the writer to the Hebrews says little about the Holy Spirit, other than as the author of Scripture (3.7; 9.8; 10.15; cf.

also 9.14); the Spirit is mentioned in passing in a list of blessings which Christians receive (6.4). The writer appears to have accepted belief in the Holy Spirit (like belief in the resurrection of Jesus, 13.20) as part of Christian tradition, but not to have developed it in any distinctively personal way, as John and Paul did.

2.5–18   *The Son and the sons*

Quite apart from what the writer actually says in this passage, the development of the letter seems to follow a pattern deeply engraved in many traditions. In classical music, a quick, joyous first movement is often followed by a slow, reflective, sadder movement. Folk tales often begin with a couple falling in love, and then have a passage in which they are overtaken by separation or some other difficulty. In Hebrews, ch.1 has been a paean of praise, celebrating the glory of the exalted Christ. The present passage is largely a flash-back to ch.1; it, traces the way of suffering which Jesus trod to reach his present glory.

From another point of view, ch.1 is concerned with Jesus' relationship as Son to his Father, whereas the present passage is concerned with his relationship to his human brothers (and by implication sisters). This double relationship will be expressed in the period leading to the Council of Chalcedon (451) in terms of the divine and human 'natures' of Christ. But in Hebrews the person of Christ (who he is) is never separated from his work (what he has done). The writer says in effect that Jesus had to be who he was in order to do what he did. In order to rescue fallen humanity from the powers of evil, he had both (1) to have the divine power which alone could break the devil's power (v. 14), and (2) to take a firm grasp on humanity by living a fully human life (vv. 16–18).

Yet even this is too static a picture to do full justice to Hebrews' thought. The writer takes time and history seriously: he believes (1) that Christ was eternally with God from the beginning of time (1.2); (2) that he took 'for a short while' (2.7) a lower status, involving testing and suffering (2.18); and (3) that because he came out of that testing triumphantly, God has given him even greater glory than he had before. And the purpose of this whole movement, from heaven to earth and back, was 'to help' other fellow human beings 'who are in the midst of their test'. 'He did it', the writer says in effect to his readers, 'for us, more precisely, for people in dangerous situations like yours.'

The central part of Hebrews (7.1 – 10.18) will explore this teaching in greater detail by describing Jesus as high priest: a human being appointed by God to overcome the barriers which sin had set up between humanity and God. This is difficult teaching, probably new to his readers, so the writer approaches it with care. The first hint of it comes in 2.17, one of the key verses of Hebrews.

1.5–14 consisted almost entirely of Old Testament quotations, with very little comment. Modern readers find problems there, asking for example by what right a text referring to Solomon (1.5b), or to some other king of Israel (1.13) can be reapplied to Christ. The writer seems to anticipate no problems with this; if he had, he would have stopped to explain and argue. In the present passage, we find him arguing through a passage which did pose a problem; and the way he deals with it is an interesting indication of how he might have dealt with problems with other texts, if they had arisen.

The main quotation, in vv. 6–8, comes from Ps. 8.5–7. On the face of it, it is about 'man' or 'a man'; the Greek means 'mankind', or 'a human being'. The psalm describes how God gave him a status not far short of that of the angels ('little less than a god' is how REB translates the Psalm), 'crowned with glory and honour', lord of creation (see Gen. 1.26). 'That's all very well', we can almost hear the writer of Hebrews saying to himself; 'the only problem is that it isn't true; it doesn't correspond with the facts. There are all kinds of (mainly evil) powers which are outside human control. So what does this text mean? There is only one man of whom it is true: Jesus. If we think of him as we read the psalm, it all becomes clear: it speaks of God's care for his Son, Christ's lowly status during his earthly life, his victory over evil, and his present glory.'

Yet the writer does not use this argument as a way of escape from the literal meaning of the text, but rather as a way of opening up still deeper truth. The text is not about humanity as it is; it is about Jesus. Yet in another sense it *is* about humanity too: humanity as it can become now that Jesus has taken hold of it to lead it back to God.

2.5 *Has subjected* anticipates 'put . . . in subjection' in v. 8. The word for *world* is the one used in 1.6, but here it is explicitly *the world to come*, the new order established by Christ.

2.6 begins, literally, 'someone testifies somewhere', by implication, in Scripture. The writer does not care who wrote the psalm, although it is in fact attributed to David: what matters is that it carries divine authority. *Solemn assurance* is a more emphatic form of a verb used elsewhere in Hebrews of the witness or testimony of Scripture (see 7.8, 17; 10.15; 11.2, 4, 5, 39; compare 3.5).

In the quotation, the psalmist is speaking of God. The second line of the quotation means practically the same as the first: *remember* implies 'care for'. *A man* is literally 'a son of man', that is, a typical or representative human being. Ezekiel is often addressed in this way by heavenly beings (for example, Ezek. 2.1,3,6,8; REB 'O man'). The title 'Son of Man', which Jesus often uses of himself, was apparently not understood outside the Hebrew and Aramaic speaking area, and is rarely used in the New Testament outside the gospels (Acts 7.56; Rev. 1.13; 14.14). The writer of Hebrews does not comment on this phrase in the psalm; he probably understood it, not as a title, but as meaning simply 'a man'.

2.7   In the psalm, the Hebrew must mean that God gave mankind a status only a little lower than the angels (or possibly 'little less than a god'). The language is spatial. The corresponding Greek may mean the same as the Hebrew, or it may mean *for a short while*. The writer of Hebrews follows the second, temporal sense; he understands the words to refer to Jesus' life on earth.

2.8   The writer heavily emphasizes the word *everything* in the psalm, in order to show that it cannot possibly apply *yet* (2.9) to anyone but Christ. Humanity has some control over the universe, but by no means total control. It is arguable that humanity has more control over the earth, if not the universe, now than it had in New Testament times, but the human situation is still fundamentally as Hebrews states it.

2.9   This first mention of Jesus by name is given tremendous emphasis by the unusual order of the Greek words: literally 'but the one "for a short while to angels subordinated" we see JESUS, because of the suffering of death "with glory and honour crowned" . . .' Jews will not pronounce God's personal name 'Yahweh'. New Testament writers have no such inhibitions about using the Greek word for 'God', and it would be going too far to suggest that the writer of Hebrews has a similar feeling for the name *Jesus*; but it is a fact that he rarely uses it on its own, and tends to keep it in reserve for great climaxes (compare 3.1; 4.14; 6.20; 7.22; 10.19; 12.2,24; 13.12). He also normally uses it in speaking of Jesus' earthly life, and especially his death.

By God's gracious will is literally 'by the grace of God'; this is the wording found in the vast majority of manuscripts, including all the oldest ones. But a few Greek manuscripts, including some used by many early church fathers, have 'without God', that is, 'apart from God' (see REB margin). If this more difficult reading is correct, it could refer to a time when Jesus felt alienated from God, either in Gethsemane (Mark 14.32–42 and parallels; compare Heb. 5.7), or on the cross (Mark 15.34 and parallels), or both.

Experience death is literally 'taste death'; a common idiom (Mark 9.1 and parallels; John 8.52). A literal translation would be too weak; GNB has simply 'die'. *For all mankind* is simply 'for everyone'.

2.10 is a compact sentence which combines various themes. In the phrase *many sons*, the word for 'son' is the same as that used of Jesus. The oldest Greek manuscripts were written entirely in capital letters, so there is no distinction in form between 'son' and 'Son'. The writer boldly uses the same word, in order to show that God's purpose for humanity is that it should share Christ's status. It does so, however, through him and in dependence on him as *the pioneer of their salvation*, the one who led the way, if not precisely to God's right hand, at least to *glory* in heaven. This kind of language has been spoiled for many people by individualist choruses of the 'that will be glory for me' type. There is no such individualism in Hebrews: no single human being, apart from Jesus, is called 'the son'; the quotations in vv. 12–13, like the great picture of heaven in 12.22–24, all refer to a community (compare the 'city' of 11.10, and the 'country' of 11.14–16). Hebrews is in line with the rest of the New Testament in emphasizing both our dependence on Christ and also the ways in which believers share in his authority (see Matt. 19.28 and parallel; John 20.22–23; I Cor. 6.2–3; Revelation).

Here the writer speaks of what was *fitting*; in 7.26 the same word is translated 'suited'. In 2.17 he will speak more strongly of what 'had' to happen. Of course this does not mean that the writer can lay down what it was right and proper for God to do. The writer, like the rest of us, can only look at what God did in fact do, and recognize that it hangs together. In particular he sees that human need was so great that nothing but what God has done in Christ could effectively meet it. This will be a major theme of Hebrews.

God is not in the Greek, but is clearly implied. *Make . . . perfect* does not mean that Jesus was morally imperfect during his earthly life: the writer states clearly in 4.15 that Jesus was tempted or tested, but did not sin. Perfection is an important and many-sided concept in Hebrews (see especially 5.9; 6.1; 7.28; 10.14; 11.40; 12.23). Here, as in most places, the main idea is that of completion. Jesus' death completed what God had sent him to earth to do. Similar language is used by Jesus in Luke 13. 32, and by Paul in II Tim. 4.7, in speaking of themselves as finishing their course on earth.

'Suffering' in Hebrews usually implies death; here *sufferings* is probably used to avoid repeating the word 'death', used in v. 9.

2.11 The writer now explores the relationship between Jesus and other human beings. He will return in v. 14 to the theme of Jesus' death.

He who consecrates is Jesus; 'those who are consecrated' are other human beings. *All of one stock* is literally 'all of one'. Grammatically, that may be either 'one person' (Abraham? Adam?) or 'one thing' (something in common, a common humanity). The latter is more likely, but there is not much difference in meaning. It is most unlikely that the words refer only to common Jewish descent (though see comment on v. 16). 'Consecrate' or 'make holy' means, negatively, to purify from sin (so GNB here), and positively, to set someone or something apart, to belong exclusively to God. The second aspect is more important, but it is impossible without the first. Hebrews will show later how Jesus by his sacrifice purified people from their sins, so that they might belong entirely to God (see especially 10.10, also 10.14,29; 13.12).

The second half of v. 11 prepares for the quotation in v. 12, pointing to its key word *brothers* (including sisters; 'men' is literally 'them'). *Does not shrink from calling* is literally 'is not ashamed to call'; it is virtually a double negative, meaning 'recognizes', almost 'is proud to acknowledge' (compare Matt. 10.32 and parallel; Mark 8.38 and parallel; Rom. 1.16; Heb. 11.16; II Tim. 1.8,12,16. The idea is expressed in Isaac Watts' hymn 'I'm not ashamed to own my Lord . . . Then will he own my worthless name . . .' (*HP* 677). Christ's recognition of those who trust him is the appropriate counterpart of believers' confession (Heb. 3.1; 4.14; 10.23) of their faith and hope in him.

2.12 *When he says,* in this context, probably means 'when Jesus (speaking in Scripture) says'; the meaning 'when it (Scripture) says' is less natural. The quotation comes from Ps. 22.22, a psalm quoted three other times in the New Testament; see Mark 15.34 and parallel, where Jesus in agony quotes the psalm's opening words; John 19.24, quoting Ps. 22.18. The present quotation comes from the happier second part of the psalm, where the psalmist has been brought through his troubles and gives thanks publicly to God. *Your fame* is literally 'your name'; the same word translated 'title' in 1.4. Here 'your fame' means 'God's fame'. *My brothers* in the psalm referred to fellow Israelites attending public worship in the Temple; but although most of the first readers of Hebrews were probably Jews, v. 11 strongly suggests that the writer intends no limitations either of race or sex. Christians were among the first to speak of one another as members of the same family, even when they were not physically related (Mark 3.32–34 and parallels; 'brothers' Rom. 1.13 and very often in Paul; James 1.2 and often; 'sister' Rom. 16.1; I Cor. 7.15; Philemon 2; James 2.15; 'mother' figuratively Rom. 16.13; 'father' Philemon 10; 'like a father' I Thess. 2.11; I Tim. 5.1; 'brother-love' Heb. 13.1).

Assembly is the word normally translated 'church'. In the psalm, it is a gathering of worshippers in the Temple. The writer of Hebrews probably thinks of God's heavenly court with its 'myriads of angels' (12.22) and believers (12.23).

2.13   The quotation is from the first lines of Isa. 8.17 and 18, which speak of secret teaching which the prophet is not yet to share even with his disciples; but Isaiah will soon (9.2) announce that

The people that walked in darkness
have seen a great light.

Perhaps the writer of Hebrews is already thinking about the 'difficult' teaching he has to give later (5.11).

The first *and again* introduces the second quotation (compare 1.6,10). The second 'and again' may be used as we would use an ellipsis (. . .), showing that part of the text has been omitted. Alternatively, it may serve to draw special attention to the second part of the quotation. Language close to the first part of v. 13 is used in II Sam. 22.3 and Isa. 12.2, but it is obviously more likely that the writer is quoting from successive verses in Isa. 8.

In any case, both halves of the quotation speak to the readers' situation. *I will keep my trust fixed on him* is for the writer of Hebrews a good description of Jesus' faithfulness to God, a faithfulness which he hopes his readers will also maintain. But the immediate point of the quotation is the word 'children' in the second half. The writer does not worry over the change from 'brothers' in v. 12 to *children* here, or argue about whether the 'children' are God's or Christ's.

The point is that Christ, in full view of God and his heavenly host, places himself in solidarity alongside believers, who are members of the same family.

2.14–15 The sentence begins with a 'therefore' which REB does not translate, since the writer is not drawing a conclusion from what he has just said, but developing the point he made in v. 11a. The *children* mentioned in the last quotation share a common humanity – and Jesus chose to share it too. (The word for 'chose' is not in the text, but the word for *shared* refers to a single event in the past.)

Now for Jesus to become a human being meant becoming mortal, subject to death, something which every human being fears. The writer does not exactly say here that Jesus also was afraid of death, but he comes close to it in 5.7. What he does say here, at least by implication, is that in dying Jesus entered a realm where evil was in control, fought the powers of evil there, and won. *Break the power of . . . the devil* may mean that Jesus destroyed the devil, or at least made him completely ineffective. As Paul puts it, Christ, and therefore those who believe in him, are 'no longer under the dominion of death' (Rom. 6.9). The writer of Hebrews will have much more to say about how this happened; it is part of his teaching method to touch gently on a subject, leave it, and return to discuss it in more detail later. For the moment, it is enough to say that those who belong to Christ have no longer any reason to fear death; it is like being set free from prison. The word for *liberate* is different from the more common word for 'salvation' or 'deliverance' used in 1.14; 2.3, but the meaning is essentially the same.

Christ's death and resurrection are thus seen as a cosmic battle between God and the devil. This picture has been used by theologians down the centuries as one way of expressing what Christ achieved. This 'Christ the conqueror' theme is particularly associated with St Anselm (Archbishop of Canterbury from 1097 until his death in 1109). The theme reappears in Martin Luther's hymn 'Christ Jesus lay in death's strong bands' (*MHB* 210):

> It was a strange and dreadful strife,
>   When Life and Death contended;
> The victory remained with Life,
>   The reign of Death was ended . . . (v.2)

2.16 *Descendants of Abraham* is probably not as racially exclusive as it sounds, for two reasons. First, not Abraham but Jacob was the ancestor of the Jews; Jacob's name was changed to Israel (Gen. 32.28; 35.10). Abraham, by contrast, was known as 'father of many nations' (Gen. 17.5). Second, 'descendants of Abraham' are contrasted with angels. This and the wider context suggest that human beings generally are meant, rather than any particular race or races.

The word for *helps* is unusual; it is twice repeated in the Greek. For a long time, it was thought to be a technical term for Christ 'taking on' human nature in addition to his divine nature. That may be how NJB ('took to himself') still understands it. It is now generally agreed, however, that the translation 'helps' (also GNB, NIV) is correct.

2.17–18   There are a few places in Hebrews where the writer compresses into a sentence ideas which will take chapters to explain in detail. This passage, a single sentence in Greek, is perhaps the greatest of these. First he gathers up the previous discussion, saying in effect: 'The reason why, as I said, Jesus had to be made like his brothers in every way was to equip him to be a merciful and faithful high priest . . .'

This introduces for the first time what will prove to be Hebrews' greatest single contribution to the understanding of who Christ was: his use of the title *high priest*. He repeats it almost immediately in 3.1, perhaps so that his readers and hearers will not forget it; the meaning of this title will be developed progressively in later chapters. No one else in the New Testament uses this title in speaking of Jesus. The writer of Hebrews well knows that Jesus was not qualified to be a priest during his earthly life (7.13; compare 8.4). John 17, however, is sometimes called Jesus' high priestly prayer, and this is a good name for it, although it does not use the title of high priest. Paul, like Hebrews, sometimes refers to Jesus' death as a sacrifice (Eph. 5.2; compare I Cor. 5.7).

Where did the writer of Hebrews get the idea of calling Jesus 'high priest'? Various answers to this question have been suggested, but the simplest and most likely is that it grew from the writer's own study of the Old Testament. Beginning from the familiar text Ps. 110.1 (quoted in Heb. 1.13), he moved first to v. 4 of the same psalm, which speaks of 'a priest according to the order of Melchizedek' (NRSV); then back in ch. 7 to the only other mention of Melchizedek in the Old Testament; and on to the conclusion that, despite belonging to the wrong tribe, or perhaps precisely because he did not descend from Levi, Jesus became high priest *par excellence* of a quite different kind from any other, offering a sacrifice which supersedes all others. 'High priest' is in fact an unusual title in the canonical Old Testament.

It is more frequent in those parts of the Apocrypha (deuterocanonical books) which were written at a time when the high priest of Israel was virtually the national leader of Israel, as in the gospels and when Hebrews was written. The Old Testament texts to which the writer of Hebrews appeals speak only of a priest. The writer of Hebrews quotes these accurately, but when he writes in his own words, he speaks of Jesus as 'high priest', no doubt to emphasize his supreme status in the new order.

All this, however, is to come. For the moment, the writer contents himself with describing this high priest, first, as 'merciful' (not a quality associated in the Bible with priests, whose work had to do more with public worship than with pastoral care) and 'faithful'. REB's *faithful as their high priest before God* shows, not only that Jesus in a general sense remained faithful to his father, but that he faithfully discharged the office to which he had been appointed – like, for example, the faithful steward in Luke 12.42.

Before God translates a set phrase meaning 'in things to do with God', particularly public worship. Hebrews constantly sees what Christ has done in terms of a new kind of worship, priesthood, and sacrifice.

To make expiation for is a single verb in Greek. Outside the Bible, it is used of doing something to God (or the gods), namely, 'propitiating' him or making him favourable to the worshipper. The translations 'make atonement for' (NIV), and especially 'turn aside God's wrath, taking away' (NIV note), find this meaning here. In this text, however, the verb is used of doing something, not to God but to sins; that is, to 'expiate' (REB, NJB), 'make expiation for' (RSV), 'make a sacrifice of atonement for' (NRSV), or 'take away' (TNT) sins; GNB translates simply 'so that the people's sins would be forgiven'. Elsewhere Hebrews says that Christ 'brought about purification from sins' (1.3), that he 'appeared . . . to abolish sin' (9.26), or 'to deal with sin' (9.28 GNB). Hebrews assumes, like other biblical writers, that sin was ultimately against God, and that therefore only God could ultimately forgive sin (see Mark 2.7 and parallels). Sacrifices, ordained by God, could be made to 'cover' or wipe out (not 'cover up'!) certain types of sin, but the worst deliberate sins could not be forgiven; the sinner must die. (For the different treatment of deliberate sins and accidental breaking of the law, see Lev. 4 and Num. 15.22–31; these passages are very important for the understanding of Hebrews.) In the following chapters, Hebrews will explore more deeply the meaning of Christ's sacrificial death for sinners, claiming that for those who 'deliberately' (10.26) reject that sacrifice there is no hope even under the new order. The writer does not stop here to explain what it is to 'expiate' sin, no doubt partly because the readers were familiar with the general idea from their study of the Old Testament, and partly because the writer has more to say about it later.

This is the only place in Hebrews where the verb translated 'expiate' is used. A related verb is used with this meaning in Zech. 7.2, where REB translates 'entreat the favour of the Lord'; similarly 8.22; in Mal. 1.9, REB translates 'placate God'. The verb used in the present verse occurs in only one other New Testament text, Luke 18.13, where a tax-collector prays: 'have mercy on me'. A related noun is used in Heb. 9.5 of the 'place of expiation' in the Temple.

2.18   In the light of the previous passage, it is clear that the supreme *test of suffering* through which Jesus passed is his death; 'suffering' in Hebrews regularly implies dying. This does not exclude other tests or temptations which Jesus underwent 'in the course of his earthly life' (5.7). These may be the temptations at the beginning of his ministry (Matt. 4.1–11 and parallel), though the writer of Hebrews does not refer to these explicitly. More probably he is thinking of the testing in Gethsemane (Heb. 5.7; compare Mark 14.32–42 and parallels). In any case he certainly has in mind the 'struggle against sin' (12.4) in which his readers are involved.

The end of this section is a good place at which to take stock, and consider how the idea of Jesus as high priest can best be understood today. The first readers knew quite well, from the Old Testament and Jewish tradition if not from personal experience, who priests and high priests were, and what they did. (Some have thought that the readers were former Jewish priests, and this theory, though unlikely, is understandable.) The first readers' problem was to understand how Jesus could be a high priest of a new and different kind. This may be a problem for Jewish readers today, and they may find Hebrews a useful guide in solving it. Christian readers today may be divided into two groups, depending on whether they describe their ministers as priests or not. The first group will have to bear in mind, if they are to understand Hebrews, that priesthood, as understood and practised in some Christian churches, corresponds neither to Old Testament priesthood, since no animal sacrifices are involved, nor to the priesthood of Christ, since that is unique. A Christian priest may be thought of as participating, in a true but dependent sense, in the priesthood of Christ; not repeating his own sacrifice, which was offered 'once for all' (9.26–28), but recalling it or representing it to God in the name of Christ. This goes further than Hebrews, which does, however, speak of Christ's continuing ministry of intercession in heaven. At no point does the writer of Hebrews give the title 'priest' to any individual but Christ (and Melchizedek who 'bears the likeness of the Son of God', 7.3); nor does he speak of Christians as being collectively 'a holy priesthood to offer spiritual sacrifices' (I Peter 2.5, compare v. 9).

If there is in Hebrews any point of contact between the work of Christ and that of Christian leaders, it appears to be in the area of pastoral care rather than that of offering sacrifice. Jesus is 'merciful and faithful' (2.17); he gives 'timely help' (4.16); 'he is able to help those who are in the midst of their test' (2.18). The same spirit seems to inspire the leaders of the church to which Hebrews is addressed: 'they are tireless in their care for you' (13.7; compare v. 7). But any link between their ministry and Christ's is not expressed; still less is there any exclusive link between Christ's priesthood and that of any separate ordained group within the church.

Christians whose ministers reject, or do not claim, the title 'priest' may find it difficult to accept it in Hebrews; it may be at best a meaningless, and at worst a negative term. Such readers will need to make the effort to lay aside their preconceptions and learn afresh, or for the first time, from the text of Hebrews what priesthood is. They too, like the first group of readers, will need to recognize that, within the new order, Hebrews applies this title to Jesus alone. They will need to put together, from all the evidence in Hebrews, a total picture of Jesus as high priest, recognizing that both his ministry and his sacrifice are presented as unique (Melchizedek is not really an exception). Then they will be able to explore, going beyond Hebrews, how the work of Christ is related to the particular tasks of any full-time ministers which their church may have; and to the ministry of the whole people of God in the world, as they present Christ to the world, and intercede for the world in the name of Christ.

3.1–6 *Jesus is greater than Moses*

It might seem to a modern reader that if Jesus is greater than the angels, he must obviously be greater than Moses, and that to say so now is an anticlimax. For the first readers, that was not necessarily so: when God gave his law to Israel, angels played a minor role in transmitting it to Moses (2.2). Moreover, what Moses did is more directly related to the argument of Hebrews than anything the angels did. It was important for the writer to begin by reaffirming what the readers already believed, namely that Christ had been raised to the right hand of God. It is even more important now to prepare the ground for showing how Jesus by his death has superseded the Old Testament sacrifices which God had set up through Moses.

This is a delicate task. Some of the readers appear to have been in danger of losing their hold on Christ, and deciding that the 'old time religion' of Moses was, after all, good enough for them. The writer is therefore careful to give due honour to Moses, as appointed by God to a special office among his people, and as pointing forward to a higher revelation which was to come. The section ends by relating this teaching once more to the readers' situation.

3.1 *Brothers in the family of God* is literally 'holy brothers'. REB shows that 'holy' means here 'belonging to God' as his children (2.13f.), and thus as brothers and sisters of one another. Just as Jesus 'shared' (2.14) in flesh and blood, so Christians share as *partners* (compare 3.14) in a *heavenly calling*. This phrase may mean (1) 'a call from heaven', that is, from God, or (2) 'a call to heaven', that is, to be with God; probably both.

Think of Jesus is similar in meaning to 'our eyes fixed on Jesus' in 12.2, though less strong. The name 'Jesus' is emphasized, as in 2.9. This is the only place in the New Testament in which Jesus is called *apostle*, a term usually kept for his closest followers. Here 'apostle' has its literal meaning of someone sent out, in this case as God's ambassador to mankind. *High priest of the faith we profess* is literally 'high priest of our confession'. The new title 'high priest', just used for the first time in 2.17, is repeated, as a good language teacher will revise new vocabulary before the students have time to forget it. But the writer insists that what the new title means is not what Paul calls 'another gospel' (Gal. 1.6–7), something different from the truth they have received. On the contrary, it is an integral part of the faith which they already profess. The word for 'faith' used so often in chapter 11 is not used here, and never refers to the content of Christian belief; Hebrews' word for that is 'confession', used also in 4.14; 10.23.

3.2 Both Jesus and Moses were *faithful* (2.17) in discharging the office to which God had appointed them; only the offices were different. In order to show how this was so, and prove that Jesus' office was superior, the writer turns to Num. 12.7, which he will quote directly in v. 5. In its Old Testament setting, the purpose of this verse is to show that Moses has a unique status. He is more than a prophet: 'of all my household', God says, 'he alone is faithful'. The writer of Hebrews bases his argument on the wording of the Greek Old Testament, literally '*in* all my house'. The word for *house* also means *household*, that is, the family and anyone else who lives with them. In Num. 12.7, it means 'household'; the writer of Hebrews has both meanings in mind. The little key word 'in' may also mean 'among', so that the whole phrase could mean 'among all the members of his [God's] household', as in Numbers. For the moment, the writer of Hebrews is content to speak of Moses in positive terms which his readers would happily accept; the contrast with Jesus will not be fully stated until v. 6.

3.3   The author's tactful approach to a delicate subject helps to make this verse slightly unclear. *Jesus* is literally 'this one' (masculine); the writer does not over-use the name of Jesus. The main point can be understood in two ways, depending on whether one thinks of a 'house' or a 'household'. In the first case, the principle involved is that someone who builds and equips a house (the Greek word covers both, though building is the main point here) is more to be respected than someone who merely works in the house. In the second case, the meaning is that someone who *founds* a family is more to be honoured than its junior members. The first interpretation fits in well with the following verses; the second would recall the 'many sons' of 2.10. In either case, Jesus enjoys higher status than Moses.

3.4   The last statement is one which the readers might have found difficult to accept; so in this verse the author first states and then applies a general principle with which they would more readily agree. The first point is a matter of common sense: every household must have had a founder, every house must have had someone to build and equip it. The second point is a matter of common belief, shared by Christians and non-Christian Jews: the 'builder' or creator of the universe is God. This already goes further than Num. 12.7, where 'my house(hold)' is Israel.

3.5f.   The conclusion of the argument comes in the form of a carefully balanced comparison and contrast between Moses and Christ:

Moses	*Christ*
was faithful	*is faithful*

in [God's] *whole household*	*as a Son*
as a servant	*over* [God's] *household*

The words in square brackets are implied. NRSV has 'Christ . . . was faithful', implying that he was faithful to death during his earthly life. Most translations have 'Christ is faithful' (or 'trustworthy', NJB), meaning that he faithfully discharged the office of Son; this is probably the point here.

The word for *servant* is used only of Moses in the Greek Bible: see Num. 11.11; 12.7.8; Ex. 14.31; Deut. 3.24. Outside the Bible, it is similarly used of someone serving a god; it does not mean 'slave'. For the writer to the Hebrews, it clearly refers to someone less important than the Son of God.

The words that God would speak, by implication 'later'. This refers back to what was said at the beginning of Hebrews about God's twofold 'speaking' in Old Testament times and in Christ. The writer of Hebrews' reinterpretation of Num. 12.7 is a good example of how he sees Old Testament texts as speaking implicitly of Christ. God waits, as it were, for Christians to discover their underlying meaning by the guidance of the Holy Spirit (compare John 5.39). This is not, for the writer, arbitrarily reading into a text something which is not there; it is a way of expressing his belief in the continuity of God's purpose throughout the history of his people. Something similar happens whenever anyone today takes an old text from any part of the Bible, and tries to apply it to his own situation. Such 're-readings' of Scripture must always be done carefully, with prayer for the guidance of the Holy Spirit, and they must be related to the original meaning, but they are a necessary final stage in understanding what the Bible says.

Set over is the author's conclusion (1) from the fact that the Old Testament only speaks of Moses as God's 'servant', 'in' his household; and (2) from the belief, previously recalled and accepted by the readers, that Jesus is God's Son.

The second half of v. 6 applies this conclusion to the readers' situation. *We are that household*: REB follows a slightly different Greek text, one less well attested than that followed by most translations, which have 'we are his house' or 'household' (NRSV, GNB, NIV, NJB). This may mean 'Christ's household', but more probably 'God's household', as in the previous verses.

But membership of God's household is not automatic: it is something which has to be held on to with courage and pride. The word for *fearless* is used also in 4.16 ('boldly'); 10.19; 10.35 ('confidence').

In John, it is used differently, of Jesus speaking 'openly', not in riddles (7.13,26; 10.24; 11.14; 16.25,29; 18.20); in Acts, it describes the characteristic freedom with which the apostles spoke in public of Christ (2.29; 4.13,29,31; 28.31). In Hebrews, the same word points on the one hand to the readers' reasons for fear, whether of death (2.15) or persecution (10.32–34; 12.3–4); and on the other hand to the free access to God in worship which Christ has now made possible (12.19; cf. w. 21–24). Yet even now the benefits which he has won for believers lie partly in the future; they are a matter of *hope*, and they can be lost. Everything depends on the readers' endurance.

3.7 – 4.13   *A rest for God's people*

The readers' need for endurance is now illustrated by a long discussion of related Old Testament texts. The most important of these, quoted at length in 3.7–11, comes from Ps. 95.7–11. On the one hand, this is a warning to the readers not to imitate Israel's repeated disobedience at the time of the exodus from Egypt (Heb. 3.16–18; compare Ex. 17.1–7; Num. 14.1–35). On the other hand, it is a promise, since it speaks of God's *rest*, which in turn recalls the seventh day of creation (Heb. 4.4; compare Gen. 2.2). Throughout this passage, which may have been first delivered as a separate sermon, the author shows his ability, not only to read an Old Testament text in the light of its immediate context, but also to move freely around the Bible. This ability is all the more remarkable since few people at that time had a complete collection of Old Testament scrolls, and reference to them was a laborious business. The memory of scholars was however better developed in ancient times, as for example among some Muslims today in recitation of the Qur'an.

3.7–11   It is grammatically possible to understand the whole quotation as falling between parentheses, so that the main sentence would run: 'That is why' (v. 7) 'you must see to it . . .' (v. 12). Since, however, the quotation forms the basis of the following argument, most translations make the quotation stand on its own. *Today* is not repeated in the Greek.

The quotation follows the Greek Old Testament fairly closely. In v. 8, it translates the proper names 'Massah' and 'Meribah' as 'rebellion' and 'testing'; the Hebrew words mean 'testing' and 'complaining'. They are alternative names for the place where Israel, needing water in the wilderness, put God to the test by asking 'Is the Lord with us or not?' (Ex. 17.7; compare Num. 20.2–13; Deut. 6.16; 9.22; 33.8; Ecclus. (Ben Sira) 6.21).

Therefore *for forty years they saw the things I did*: the psalm, in both Hebrew and Greek, takes the words 'for forty years' with the next verse: 'For forty years I abhorred that generation.' In the Old Testament setting, the 'forty years' are the period of wandering in the wilderness before taking possession of the promised land. In Hebrews, there is no such limitation on the period of God's anger with those who fall away from faith (but see comment on 3.17). It is not certain whether 'the things I did' are good things for which the Israelites should have been grateful, or bad things which should have been a warning to them; in Hebrews, probably the latter.

Hebrews' comment on this passage takes up the rest of ch. 3, not to mention the repeated quotations in 4.3,7. The comment is nevertheless selective: the key words for Hebrews come at the beginning, 'today', and the end, 'my rest'. *Today*, as the writer explains in v. 13, means not one particular day, but any 'today' on which God speaks to his people in the words of the psalm. But neither is it an unlimited period. If the possibility of listening and responding to what God is saying remains open, so also does the possibility of finally rejecting his message. *Enter my rest* suggests not a state of rest, but rather a (heavenly) place of rest: something which the writer will later call a heavenly 'country' or 'city' (11.16); in other words, heaven, viewed as a place where God is, and where his people can remain secure.

3.12   The author does not issue a blanket condemnation of all his readers: he calls on them to carry out a kind of spiritual 'neighbourhood watch' (compare 12.12–13; 13.3), to see that no single member of their community is lost. The danger is described as having, literally, 'an evil heart of unbelief', REB a *wicked and faithless heart*. Here, as in the Old Testament, the heart is thought of, not merely as the seat of the emotions, but the centre of the human personality, especially its will. So any loss of faith among the readers would not be a mere passing fit of depression, but a deliberate and sustained act of rebellion (vv. 15–16). The Greek word translated *deserter* is literally 'fall away', a word from which the English word 'apostasy' comes. *The living God* probably means in Hebrews, not only that the Lord is the only God who is truly alive, but that he is the only source of life (see also 4.12; 9.14; 10.31), so that to fall away from him is death.

3.13 'The word of God', as the writer will say later (4.12), 'is alive and active', not only to judge but also to encourage. The word translated 'appeal' in 13.22 may be translated 'encouragement'; this is the main purpose of Hebrews. So every day on which the 'today' of Ps. 95 is heard, it is to be understood as God's encouraging appeal to the hearts and wills of those who hear; and God's word in Scripture is to be backed up by believers' encouraging appeals to one another (*encourage one another*, 3.13). In the same way, the public reading and private study of the Bible today interact with pastoral care. (Nothing is said here about the special responsibilities of church leaders, on which see 13.17.) *No one of you* is emphatic. 'Made stubborn' is literally 'hardened', because the hardening of the heart is a matter of the will. *Wiles* is simply 'deceit': 'in order that none of you be deceived by sin' (GNB).

3.14 largely repeats 3.6:

3.6	*3.14*
We are	*We have become*
that household,	*partners with Christ,*
if only	*if only*
we are fearless	*we keep our initial confidence*
and keep our hope high.	*firm to the end.*

To be members of God's household is the same as to be 'partners' (3.1) with (or of) Christ; but both depend on remaining faithful to the end.

3.15 repeats the first two lines of the quotation (Ps. 95.7–8; Heb. 3.7–8). REB is probably right in linking this quotation with what follows, as does NJB; RSV links it with v. 14, and GNB, NIV and NRSV make it a separate sentence. As vv. 17–18 will show, repetition of the first part of the quotation is meant to remind the readers of the whole passage.

3.16–18 In fine preaching style, the writer brings out the message of the psalm in three pairs of rhetorical questions: basically:

Who was it . . . ?   Was it not those who . . . ?

The language varies a little to avoid monotony, and the questions point in turn to the beginning, middle, and end of the quotation. Once more, after touching a sensitive spot in v. 14, the writer skilfully retreats to safer statements about the Israelites in the wilderness. The direct probing of the readers' own situation will begin again in ch. 4.

But by this time, the readers must know that the writer is also speaking indirectly about them. It is not just the ancient Israelites who *heard and yet rebelled* (v. 16); the readers have also heard the gospel (2.1 and especially 4.2), but some at least of them are in danger of rejecting it. It is not just the exodus generation with whom God was angry for forty years (v. 17); the readers are in danger of coming to an equally bad end. The second part of v. 17 recalls Num. 14.29; *fell* implies 'fell down dead' (GNB). Here, in contrast to vv. 9–10, the writer is following the standard Greek and Hebrew text of the psalm. It is not just those who disobeyed or refused to believe (the Greek means both) who missed entering God's place of rest; the readers are in the same danger. This last point will be expanded in ch. 4.

It is interesting to note that the writer of Hebrews bases his appeal, not directly on the historical accounts of Israel's escape from Egypt, but on a psalm which itself refers back those events. The psalmist, and successive generations of worshippers who sung the psalm in the Temple, lived at a time when the promised land had long been won; the punishment which excluded from the promised land everyone who set out from Egypt, except Caleb and Joshua (Num. 14, especially vv. 29–34), lay far in the past. But the bitter memory remained as a permanent warning. The writer of Hebrews sees it as a warning against losing the hope of entering an eternal, heavenly promised land which God has kept open for his people (compare John 14.2–3).

3.19   summarizes the lesson drawn from the psalm: *unbelief* is the key word. The original question 'Is God in our midst or not?' (Ex. 17.7), and the complaints which went with it, show the Israelites' failure to trust God when the going got tough. The going is beginning to get tough for the readers of Hebrews; the writer does not want them to take the same disastrous course.

4.1f.   mark a further step in the same argument, rather than a fresh start. The ground is more sensitive, and perhaps for this reason (as for example in Rom. 1.12–13) the language becomes more complicated.

4.1   It is still, however, positive: God's *promise* of a place of *rest remains open* (compare 3.13), and not one (compare 3.12) of the readers will miss entering it, if the writer can prevent it. Once again, he uses 'we' forms, placing himself alongside his readers. The word *promise* recalls the idea of the promised land. The word for *missed his opportunity* is the same which Paul uses in Rom. 3.23 of being 'deprived' of the divine glory.

4.2   The comparison between the ancient Israelites and the readers is now pressed home. 'We', like 'them', were told good news, literally 'were evangelized'. In the case of the exodus generation, it was *the good news* of an earthly promised land. In the case of the readers of Hebrews, it is the Good News about Jesus (compare 2.1–4; also I Thess. 2.13). But it is not enough to hear good news; for the news to do any good it has to be trusted, accepted as true, and obeyed (5.9). The Greek word for 'obey' is related to the word for 'hear', and in some places 'hear' implies 'obey'.

This may be so here, but the manuscripts differ. REB, like RSV text, GNB, and NIV text, follow the easier reading, which means that the word which the ancient Israelites heard was not *combined with faith*, that is, did not meet with faith, in those who heard it. But most of the best manuscripts have a harder reading which NJB text translates 'they did not share the faith of those who did listen' (so RSV note, NIV note); this may well be correct.

4.3ff.   REB's *because* is not in the text, which may be translated: 'For it is we who do believe who enter the place of rest . . .' This raises a question which will occur at several places in Hebrews, and also in other parts of the New Testament (for example, Mark 1.15 and parallels). Does the writer think of believers as already enjoying what God has promised them, or do they still have to wait for it? Generally speaking, the answer is that the writer believes that the complete fulfilment of God's purpose is 'drawing near' (10.25); the old order is 'becoming obsolete and growing old', and 'will shortly disappear' (8.13). Especially in worship, Christians have what Paul called the 'firstfruits' (Rom. 8.23) or the 'pledge' (II Cor. 1.22) of what is to come. But they are not quite there yet: the verb which REB translates 'have come to' in Heb. 12.18,22 really means 'have approached'. This means that there is still room both for hope (3.6), and conversely for fear (4.1).

The second half of v. 3 contains a rather awkward twist in the argument, the reason for which will not become completely clear until vv. 9–10. The immediate point is that Ps. 95.11, now quoted for the third time, speaks about a place of *rest*. The tone, however, is now encouraging, not threatening as in 3.16–17, and in the original psalm. What is this 'place of rest'?, the author asks, arguing here as often in a way later used by other Jewish writers, including to some extent the people who wrote the Dead Sea Scrolls. It cannot have anything to do with God's rest on the seventh day of creation, because that is long past, as Gen. 2.2 (quoted in v. 4) proves.

He has said in v. 3, referring to God, and *Scripture . . . says* in v. 4, are the same in Greek. The author probably did not bother about the distinction; *somewhere* (compare 2.6) suggests that he has more important things to do than give precise references. The form of the verb, however, suggests that what God says in Scripture has permanent validity.

For good measure, in v. 5 the writer quotes Ps. 95.11 yet again, making now the point that although, on one level, Gen. 2.2 appears to contradict the psalm, on a deeper level the two texts reinforce one another. In other words, the meaning of the Genesis verse is not exhausted in the creation story: it has meaning still for us.

4.6f.   The argument now becomes rather tortuous for a modern reader, but it holds together perfectly well on the author's assumption that, within God's purpose, the words of scripture apply not only in the past but in the present. (Remember that what we call the Old Testament was the only Bible the New Testament writers had, and they took it with absolute seriousness.) The steps in the argument are as follows:

1.   Scripture proves that there is still something called 'God's place of rest'.
2.   He intends some people to come and share it with him.
3.   The exodus generation, who were the first to hear this good news, refused to listen to it, so they missed their chance of entering God's place of rest.
4.   God's intention (point 2) remains the same; so he reissues his promise, in David's psalm, to a later generation.

4.8f.   The writer, however, contrary to what one might expect, shows no interest in David's generation: his main concern is with the exodus generation and his own, with a side-glance to the creation story. Joshua led Israel into the promised land; but this was not a real fulfilment of God's promise, or the words of Ps. 95, spoken later by God, would have no meaning. On the contrary, there is still a *sabbath rest* (a word probably coined by the writer, on the basis of Gen. 2.2) for *the people of God*. It is remarkable how, despite all the criticism of the old order which will come later in Hebrews, the writer never speaks of the church as a new people of God, different from the old. He has the same loyalty to his Jewish roots which Paul expresses, in quite different terms, in Rom. 9.1–5. The name 'Joshua' is the same as 'Jesus' in Greek, but this is probably not significant for the message of Hebrews.

4.10   is another summing-up verse, rather like 3.19. To enter God's place of rest means what it says: *rest from work*, like God's on the seventh day of creation. *Work*, literally 'works', was mentioned in v. 4, quoting Gen. 2.2. Hebrews elsewhere refers both to 'good works' (10.24; 13.21; compare 6.1) and 'dead works' (6.1; 9.14); the latter phrase probably means 'acts which lead to death'. Hebrews does not, however, contrast justification by grace and by works, as Paul does. It is possible that in the present verse, the writer is already thinking of the rituals which had to be performed again and again under the old order (10.1–4), and even then were not effective. But it is more likely that at this stage, the meaning is simply that those who enter God's place of rest have no more work to do.

4.11   partly overlaps with vv. 1f.; the language is different, but the underlying appeal is the same. *Make every effort* is appropriate language for people who 'have proved so slow to learn' (5.11), and are in danger of becoming 'lax' (6.12). *No one* expresses the same concern as that expressed in 3.12 and 4.1, that not one of the readers should be lost (compare John 17.12). All members of the community must care for each, as the writer cares for them all. *Old* is implied: the last words of v. 11 are a farewell glance at the exodus generation.

4.12–13   Theologians sometimes distinguish between three forms of *the word of God*, that is, three ways in which God speaks: (1) through his Son, the incarnate word; (2) through Scripture, the written word; and (3) through preaching, the spoken word. These distinctions are useful as far as they go, though they are not absolute: the written word points to Christ (John 5.39; Acts 17.11), and most of the Bible was spoken before it was written down. But in these verses the writer of Hebrews typically fuses all three forms of God's word with one another and with God himself. No doubt he is thinking primarily of the written word, in particular the repeated 'today' of Ps. 95, which still calls men and women to come and share God's place of rest. But his own words are an effective preacher's appeal, and in their turn have become Scripture for Christians; and immediately after these verses, he begins a fresh section of teaching about who Jesus is.

It is difficult to know exactly when the writer stops talking about God's word, and begins talking about God himself. REB and other translations are almost certainly right in making the transition at the end of v.12, but the first *him* in v. 13 could theoretically be 'it'. The word of God, after all, is God speaking to his people.

4.14 – 5.10   *Jesus the great high priest*

Modern preachers are normally taught to arrange their material under clearly distinct headings, so that attentive listeners know where they are at any given point in the sermon. The writer of Hebrews follows a rather different, possibly less 'Western', strategy, one which probably demands even greater skill. The argument has a number of different phases, but these overlap and interweave in such a way that the reader or hearer is drawn smoothly from one to the next. The present verses are a good example of such a transition. On the one hand, as the opening *therefore* shows, the writer sums up and reinforces what has gone before, repeating in different words the appeal to hold fast which he has given in 3.6, 14. But on the other hand, these verses mark an important step closer to the central theme of Christ's high priesthood, which until now has been mentioned only in passing (2.17; 3.1). Notice particularly how the old, well-known title *Son of God* is placed quietly alongside the new title *high priest*, in the same way as two parts of a broken bone are set by a skilful surgeon, and left to knit together. The new joint will be soon reinforced by Scripture in 5.5–6.

High priest is one word in Greek, literally 'archpriest': so *great high priest* is emphatic, not repetitious as it may sound in English.

This high priest is close both to God and to humanity. He is close to God because of his exaltation (1.3–4, 13); he *has passed through the heavens*. Many ancient writers thought of a number of 'heavens', like the circles in Dante's *Paradise*, or Paul's 'third heaven' (II Cor. 12.2, which GNB translates 'the highest heaven'). The writer of Hebrews shows no interest in describing different heavens separately. The plural 'heavens' may indirectly reflect the dual form of the Hebrew word for heaven; similarly Matthew normally speaks of 'the kingdom of the heavens', rather than 'the kingdom of God'. Hebrews' point is simply that Jews has made the journey from earth to the highest 'place' in heaven.

Though Jesus is now seated at God's right hand, he remains also close to humanity because of the experience he gathered during his earthly life – especially the trials, tests or temptations which he successfully endured without falling into sin. This double 'nearness' to God and to humanity shows the limits of spatial language in describing personal relationships, especially with God.

The writer does not refer openly to any particular trial, so we do not know for certain whether he is thinking of the wilderness temptations at the beginning of Jesus' ministry, or (as probably in 5.7) of Gethsemane, of the cross, or of Jesus' earthly life as a whole. Nor does the writer claim any special knowledge of the events of that earthly life. But his picture of Jesus as high priest (compare 2.17) almost certainly owes something to the traditions he had received about the kind of man Jesus was; in particular his gentleness in dealing with sinners (see, for example, Mark 2.15–17 and parallels; 5.19; 10.47 and parallels; John 8.1–11).

Put the two together, and Jesus is seen as one who has both the power and the willingness to help weak human beings, such as the first readers, in their struggle against sin (compare Heb. 12.4).

The word translated *sympathize* is the Greek word from which the English 'sympathize' comes; it has the stronger meaning of 'suffering with', 'feeling our weaknesses with us' (NJB). It is related to the word translated 'bear patiently with' in 5.2.

The word translated *approach* is used several times in Hebrews; never, as often in the synoptic gospels and Acts, of literal movement, of someone coming up to someone else, but always of worshippers 'drawing near', either to the altar in the Temple (10.1), or to God (11.6; 12.18, 22f), or through Jesus as high priest to God (7.25, and by implication in 10.22 and the present verse). *The throne of grace* is God's throne, since God is the ultimate source of grace (2.9): but it is a throne which he shares with the exalted Christ (1.8). The readers are to approach this throne *boldly* (compare 3.6), relying on what Christ has done for them as their high priest. 'Timely help' is 'help . . . just when we need it' (GNB). This is the positive counterpart of Luke's statement, at the end of his story of Jesus' first temptations, that the devil 'left him until an opportune time' (Luke 4.13 NIV).

5.1–10   The writer turns to explain in greater detail the human and divine aspects of Jesus' ministry as high priest. The two qualifications of any high priest, whether of the old or the new order, are that he must be (a) *taken from among men*, and (b) *appointed* by God. In discussing both these conditions, the writer probably has in mind

Ex. 28.1, where God says to Moses: 'Out of all the Israelites you are to summon to your presence your brother Aaron and his sons to serve as my priests . . .' The order was taken to apply to all Aaron's male descendants, while other descendants of Levi (called 'levites') were later given subordinate functions in the Temple.

Heb. 5.1–4 state the qualifications for being a high priest in general terms, and vv. 5–10 apply them to Christ, but in the reverse order.

5.1 The implied subject of both *taken* and *appointed* is God: the writer is not concerned with the human beings who played a part in the choice and consecration of high priests under the old order. The word for *men* means 'human beings', not 'males'. It is a historical fact that all Israelite priests were men; indeed even women worshippers were segregated in an outer court of the Temple. But debates about women's ministry lie beyond the writer's horizon; his point is that, in order to minister to human beings, the high priest must himself be human. *Their representative before God* brings out the meaning of the set phrase translated 'before God' in 2.17. 'In matters related to God' (NIV) is a more literal translation.

The essential function of a high priest is to offer *gifts and sacrifices for sins*. In the system of worship based on the Old Testament and centred on the Temple in Jerusalem, not all sacrifices were 'for sins'. There were, for example, thank-offerings, but the writer of Hebrews is much less interested in these (he mentions spiritual sacrifices in 13.14f.). Nor does he show any interest in the distinction between animal 'sacrifices' and other 'gifts', for example of grain: his main concern is with animal sacrifices as pointing towards the sacrifice of Christ (compare 9.22). In particular, as will appear especially in ch. 9, the writer's interest concentrates on the liturgy of the great annual Day of Atonement. This selective interest in Temple worship is one of the things which suggest that the writer came, not from the land of Israel itself, but from a Jewish community of the 'dispersion'; I Peter 1.1 similarly speaks of Christians as 'the scattered people of God'.

5.2 In this verse the writer's picture of Jesus as 'merciful' (see 2.17; 4.15) seems to spill over into his picture of high priests in general. To be *able to bear patiently with the ignorant and erring* is not, however, a basic qualification for being a high priest; it follows from being human. More realistically, the high priest is 'beset by weakness'. In fact, some high priests were notorious collaborators with foreign powers, which was the main reason for the breakaway movement at Qumran. The writer, however, takes a distant and somewhat idealized view of events in Israel; it is unlikely that he knew any high priests personally.

The words 'ignorant', 'erring' and 'weakness' are carefully chosen to cover both the old high priests and Jesus; they fall short of mentioning sin, since Jesus has just been stated to be 'without sin' (4.15). 'Ignorant' does not refer to a general lack of education, but to not knowing in every detail the provisions of the law of Moses, and therefore being liable to infringe them unintentionally (see Lev. 4; Num. 15.24–29). 'Erring' means much the same, but may also cover a situation in which someone accidentally incurred ritual uncleanness, for example by touching a dead body (compare Heb. 9.7). These are the only kinds of 'sin' which, when it comes to the point, the writer will admit that the Old Testament sacrifices could deal with (see 9.10). In fact, the Old Testament ritual claimed to do more than that, but not to deal with the most serious types of sin. On the high priest's 'weakness' see 7.28. The earthly high priests were mortal (7.23) and therefore could not deal permanently with sin, as Jesus has done.

5.3   The writer now reaches the limits of what can be said in the same breath about the old high priests and Jesus. Jesus' death was indeed a 'sin-offering', but not 'for himself', like the animal sacrifices offered by the earthly high priest. *Because of this* means 'because of his weakness'. *The people* on one level means the congregation in the temple, but on another level includes the continuing people of God under what the writer will later call the new 'covenant', first mentioned in 7.22.

5.4   The other qualification for being a high priest is divine appointment. The appointment of high priests was often contested, but this was usually because they had been appointed by Greek or Roman rulers, rather than because they had tried to seize the office for themselves. The writer may not know or care much about contemporary events in Israel, but he is clear that high priests are made by God, not by any human authority. *Just as Aaron was* refers again to Ex. 28.1.

5.5f.   In these two verses, as important as any since 2.17, the writer does three things. First, he begins to apply to Jesus what has just been said about high priests in general. Second, he links (more strongly than in 4.14) the titles of Son and high priest. Third, he provides scriptural support for using them jointly of Christ.

Christ did not seize the office of high priest: God appointed him. The language is different from that of Phil. 2.6, and the title in question there is that of 'Lord'; but the underlying thought is similar. The same God who in Ps. 2.7 (already quoted in 1.5) named him 'Son' also now, in Ps. 110.4, names him high priest. The two texts are themselves linked: they come from psalms quoted at the beginning and the end of the series of texts quoted in ch. 1. The implication for the readers is clear. If, as they do, they acknowledge Jesus as Son of God, they must also acknowledge him as high priest, even though the second idea may be new and 'difficult to explain' (5.11).

The quotation of Ps. 110.4 is not explained at this stage; it will be quoted again in 6.20; 7.17. The first mention of Melchizedek, like the second in 5.10, is like a single note played in an orchestra by an instrument which will have an important solo part to play in chapter 7. There, the figure of Melchizedek will be used as a pointer to what makes Christ's priesthood different from that of the old order; but that stage in the argument is still to come. The traditional translation *in* or *after the order of Melchizedek*, found also in REB and other modern translations, is probably misleading; still more so is 'in the line of succession to Melchizedek', the second translation offered in GNB note. The writer will state in 7.3 (cf. 7.25 REB margin) that both Christ and Melchizedek are priests *for all time*; any idea of succession is therefore quite out of place. It is more likely that the meaning is simply that both Christ and Melchizedek are priests of the same kind, different from the levitical priests; the first translation in GNB note, 'like Melchizedek', is probably the correct one.

5.7–10   forms a single sentence in Greek. Some have thought that it is based on a primitive Christian hymn, but this cannot be proved. Two things are closer to certainty. First, the language recalls that of those psalms which are classified as individual laments, though they are not directly quoted. Second, here, more strongly than in 2.17 and 4.15, the writer is thinking of the earthly life of Jesus, including his death, as a time of testing or trial.

The passage is not primarily theological: the writer is fixing his eyes on Jesus, as he will later tell the readers to do (12.2). Yet several important theological concepts are touched on in passing.

(1) *In the course of his earthly life* is literally 'in the days of his flesh', recalling 2.14.

(2) *Deliver him from death* also recalls the cosmic struggle with 'him who had death at his command, that is, the devil' (2.14). It is not

41

certain whether, in the present verse, 'deliver him from death' means (a) 'deliver him out of death', that is, by resurrection; or (b) 'prevent him from dying', referring to Jesus' prayer in Gethsemane: 'Take this cup from me. Yet not my will but yours' (Mark 14.36). (a) is simpler; (b) would mean that Jesus prayed to God, who had the power, if he had wanted to use it, to prevent him from dying; and this is difficult.

(3) *Offered up* repeats a word used in 5.1.3, and several times later in Hebrews. Almost always, it refers to offering sacrifices. The writer is hinting at what he will say in detail later about Christ's death as the uniquely effective sacrifice.

(4) The word translated *devotion* in v. 7 is translated 'reverence' in 12.28; NIV and NRSV have 'reverent submission' here. RSV translated 'godly fear', but it is not the common word for fear used in 2.15, and it is unlikely that it refers to Jesus' fear of death.

(5) The words for *learned* and *sufferings* in v. 8 are similar in Greek (*emathen/epathen*). Similar plays on words are found in secular Greek writers. The theme of suffering as a sign of true sonship will be developed in 12.5–11, but there with the readers, not Jesus, directly in mind. The theme of Jesus' own obedience in death will be most fully expressed in 10.5–10. Here, in v. 9, the link is with those who in their turn obey Jesus. As one old commentator put it, 'his obedience draws ours after it.'

(6) *Once perfected*, here as elsewhere in Hebrews, means 'once his mission was completed', through death and in his exaltation (compare 12.2).

Verse 10 rounds off this phase of the argument by recalling God's words in Ps. 110.4, quoted in v. 6.

5.11 – 6.12   *There is no standing still*

This passage is almost as remarkable for what it does not say as for what it does. Like 3.7–4.13, it contains only passing mention of Christ (6.1, 6); but unlike the earlier passage, it is not based on any Old Testament passage either. The writer is appealing to his readers in his own words.

These verses therefore tell us something about the readers' situation: not indeed about their outward circumstances, but about the spiritual danger which threatens them. Earlier he has defined this danger as that of apostasy or falling away from faith in Christ (3.12;

4.11). Here it becomes clear that any such desertion was, in the writer's view, likely to come, not from sudden and unexpected crisis, but as the result of a stagnation or gradual decline. No doubt the danger was all the greater if it was likely to creep on the readers unawares.

More precisely, the readers seem unwilling to grow in the faith. They have accepted a set of elementary teachings (6.1f.) which are so general that scholars do not even agree on whether they are distinctively Christian teachings at all, or beliefs which Jews could in some sense also accept. They want, indeed the author admits that they *need* (5.12) someone to go over this elementary teaching with them again and again. They are unable or unwilling to share their faith with those less experienced than themselves, though it is time they did. Yet, if (as is surely likely) 6.4f. are not abstract statements, but are written with the readers in mind, these are people who have indeed *been enlightened . . . have tasted the heavenly gift and . . . shared in the Holy Spirit, . . . experienced the goodness of God's word and the spiritual power of the age to come . . . '* They are real Christians, a community among whom God has been at work (compare 2. 3f.; 10.32ff.; 13.7).

So what is the problem? We cannot be sure. One possibility, which would cover the facts we do have, is that the readers were gradually coming to undervalue the new thing that God had done in Christ, and settle back into their old ways of thinking, worshipping, and living. From our point of view, we might say that they had failed to realize that Christianity was a completely new religion, not just a fresh variety of Judaism. But that is not how the writer sees it: partly, of course, because he could not foresee how the church would develop in separation from Judaism, but still more because neither he nor the majority of his readers would have wanted that to happen. (The writer never uses the words 'Jew' and 'Gentile', perhaps, in contrast with Paul, to avoid calling attention to differences of race and background among his readers.) The readers were mostly what we would call 'Jewish Christians', or what many Jewish Christians today prefer to call 'Messianic Jews'. That was the readers' strength, the depth of their roots; but also their danger. To put it again in modern terms, did their loyalty to their old, safe past mean that their Christianity was to be merely adjectival; an optional extra, even?

The writer is in no doubt about the answer. They cannot stand still; they must move either forward or back. There is no halfway house for those who have once known Christ; no fall-back position. The readers cannot un-know Christ, or undo what he has done among

43

them. To attempt to ignore what God has done through his Son is to reject the 'living God' himself (3.12). More even than that, it is to renew in the present the humiliation which Jesus endured on the cross (6.6). Their final condition will be worse than the state in which they began (compare Luke 11.24–27). The only alternative is to go forward into the kind of mature Christian faith which Hebrews is written to commend. And the heart of this faith is teaching about Jesus' high priestly ministry and his sacrifice of himself.

This passage moves smoothly through three main phases, corresponding broadly to the three paragraphs in REB. First, the writer complains of his readers' spiritual immaturity (5.11–14). Next, he warns in the strongest terms of what happens to any who have *fallen away* (6.1–8). Finally, he speaks in more positive tones of what he still hopes for the readers (6.9–12).

5.11   *About Melchizedek* is literally 'about this'; and 'this' may refer to a person or a thing. It is true that the author has *much to say* about Melchizedek (see 7.1–10), and that it is *difficult to explain*. But Melchizedek is only brought in as a way of exploring what it means to say that Christ is a 'high priest in the order of', or 'like Melchizedek'. It is therefore probably better to translate 'on this subject' (NJB) or 'about this matter' (GNB).

Many modern readers will agree that this teaching is 'difficult'; but what the writer actually says is not that it is difficult in itself, but that it is hard for him to explain it to the readers, because they have become spiritually insensitive. The phrase translated *slow to learn* is literally 'hard of hearing', and the word for 'hard' is translated 'lax' in 6.12. This repetition, as often in Hebrews, helps to mark the passage as a separate section. The meaning of the repeated word varies somewhat between 5.11 and 6.12, but in both places conveys a general impression of sluggishness and insensitivity. It is the opposite of the eager listening to God's word to which the readers have been encouraged in 3.7–4.12; a defect both of understanding and of will. The language suggests a settled state, difficult to change; one not unknown in Christian communities today.

The ABC of God's oracles is literally 'the elements of the beginning of the words of God'; 'elements of the beginning' says the same thing twice for emphasis. The contrast between milk for babies and solid food for adults is found in secular writers also. The reference is to the simple truths which the readers learned first; it is natural to think of these as including the doctrines listed in 6.1–2.

5.13 *What is right* is literally 'a word of righteousness'. The writer is not thinking, as Paul does when he uses similar language, about the message of justification by faith (see the comment on 10.38); so NJB's 'the doctrine of saving justice' probably says too much. 'Righteousness' here, as typically in Matthew, means simply 'what God requires'.

5.14 'Adults' (NIV 'the mature') is the word which in 9.11 is translated 'perfect'. The underlying idea is that of completeness; here, physical maturity is used as a metaphor for maturity in faith. But spiritual maturity, as the readers' stagnation shows, does not come automatically with the passage of time. Adults' perceptions require to be *trained by long use*, as a musician practises on his instrument, or as an athlete (compare 12.1) practises in training for his sport. The purpose of this training is to develop the power to judge between right and wrong. (This is why Paul, in I Cor. 6.1–6, fails to understand why Christians should want to appeal to a pagan court.)

6.1–3 What in 5.12 was called 'the elements of the beginning of the words of God' is now called, perhaps for variety, *the rudiments of Christianity*, literally 'the word of the beginning of Christ'. Some have thought that this refers, not to Jesus, but to Jewish teaching about the Messiah. It is true that all the six beliefs mentioned can be understood without reference to Christianity (see below). It is more likely, however, that NEB and other translations are right in seeing here a reference to elementary Christian teaching; but this is not the heart of the gospel as summarized, for example, in I Cor. 15.3f. The writer is concentrating on beliefs which were not revolutionized when the readers became Christians: they were able to carry them on from their Jewish past. He should not have *to be laying the foundation all over again*. In saying this, he is not thinking of any specific heresy. There is no question, as perhaps at Corinth, of someone laying any 'other foundation than . . . Jesus Christ' (I Cor. 3.11).

The six elementary beliefs are apparently grouped in three pairs. *Repentance from the deadness of our former ways*, literally 'repentance from dead works', probably means, not only useless actions, but evil behaviour which leads to death (compare 9.14). *Cleansing rites* is probably the correct translation of a word which is literally 'baptisms', and which probably refers to repeated ritual washings practised in Judaism (see Judith 12.7ff.), as in other traditions. Less probably, it may refer to the baptism of a number of Christians, or to Christian baptism together with Jewish cleansing rites.

The laying on of hands was practised as a sign of imparting blessing or spiritual gifts (Gen. 48.17f.; Matt. 19.13; Acts 8.17ff.); in healing (Mark 5.23; II Cor. 5.11); and in ordination or commissioning for a special task (Num. 27.18; Acts 6.6; I Tim. 4.14).

It is clear from the gospels (Mark 12.18 and parallel) that by the time of Jesus, most though not all Jews believed in *the resurrection of the dead*. This belief arose towards the end of the Old Testament period (Dan. 12.2), and developed rapidly in the period between the Old and New Testaments. The writer of Hebrews, unlike Paul (for example in I Cor. 15), does not link this belief explicitly with the resurrection of Jesus, to which he refers in passing in 13.20.

REB rightly transfers *let us advance towards maturity* (see 5.14) from the beginning of 6.1 to the end of v. 2, thus linking it with v. 3. This makes better sense than to take *so we shall* as meaning that the writer agrees, after all, to 'lay . . . the foundation all over again'.

6.4ff.   This is one of the two most severe warning passages in Hebrews; the other is 10.26–31. There is nothing quite so threatening anywhere else in the New Testament, which may be the main reason why Hebrews took so long to be accepted into the Bible of the church in Western Europe.

The situation there was complicated by the fact that in the fourth century the church faced the problem of what to do with people who had renounced their faith under persecution, but later repented and wished to be readmitted to communion. The official decision was to readmit such people on certain conditions; but a group called the Donatists broke away because they refused to take communion from bishops and priests who in the past had renounced their faith. Similar problems have arisen in modern times in the wake of movements hostile to Christianity.

Hebrews' warnings are difficult for many Christians to accept, because they seem to place a limit on God's willingness to forgive (contrast Matt. 18.22). The following comments may help towards understanding. (1) The writer of Hebrews is clearly not referring to sins in general, but to wilful denial of the faith. (2) Nor is he referring to people who have superficially assented to Christianity without really understanding what it is about. He heaps up phrases to emphasize that he is speaking of Christians in the fullest sense. (3) He does not say, here or anywhere else, that any of his readers have in fact abandoned their faith. He is issuing a warning, not making a statement of fact. (4) There is nothing arbitrary about his argument: such people, he says, cannot recover their faith because they cannot repent, and repentance is the door through which one enters into faith. (5) The author's pessimism about those who reject Christ, after having once accepted him, is the negative counterpart of his conviction that Christ has offered once for all the one effective sacrifice for sin (9.26, 28). There is no other sacrifice; so the writer is expressing as a negative statement the disciples' rhetorical question: 'Lord, to whom shall we go? Your words are words of eternal life' (John 6.68). This is the most important point, and one to be borne in mind in approaching the heart of the problem (see below).

When all this has been said, these passages remain difficult. Various attempts have been made to explain them. (1) Some have claimed that no one who has truly believed in Christ can completely abandon his faith: 'once a Christian, always a Christian'. If so, the situation which the writer of Hebrews fears could never arise. If someone does abandon his faith, it shows he was never truly a Christian; if he is truly a Christian, that shows that he has not really abandoned his faith. But this is arguing in a circle and going beyond the evidence of Scripture. (2) Others have thought that the writer of Hebrews does not mean what he says. If, they say, apostates did come back and ask to be readmitted, he would welcome them with open arms. But this is speculation. The writer does not say that he would not personally be willing to receive such people back, but that it is 'impossible' for them to repent. ('Impossible' is one of his favourite words; see also 6.18; 10.4; 11.6.) (3) Still others have come to the conclusion that the writer does mean what he says, but that he is wrong. This is clearly a last resort; a modern reader would need very strong evidence for questioning a New Testament writer's understanding of any aspect of Christianity. Yet one may perhaps ask whether, if the writer had given as large a place as Paul does to the effects of Christ's resurrection, or had had so vivid a sense of the personal activity of the Holy Spirit as Paul and John, he might not have drawn such absolutely negative conclusions from his positive faith in Christ's unique sacrifice. It may be that his sense of this uniqueness makes him afraid lest his readers' faith fall back into something like the repeated rites of the old order (10.3). Other New Testament writers express the belief that Christ's sacrifice, itself unique, is effective not only in relation to the believer's past life, but also for the future (see I John 2.1f.). Hebrews, too, (7.25) speaks of Christ's continuing ministry of intercession, as Paul also writes in Rom. 8.26f., 34 about the intercession of the Holy Spirit. It must be admitted, however, that none of these passages speak specifically about apostasy.

6.7–8   The rest of this passage is both easier to understand and more encouraging. First, the writer unusually recounts a little parable, based on Gen. 3.17f. The growth of crops is an image of growth in faith, and both are signs of God's blessing. The converse is also true: lack of growth, failure to produce useful crops, is a sign of God's curse. The thought that good living normally brings prosperity runs right through the Old Testament (see for example Ps. 107; Hebrews 11.16, 38 may allude to Ps. 107.4). The Book of Job (see C. S. Rodd's commentary in this series) is an attempt to grapple with the fact that this does not always happen. The New Testament, too, often speaks of natural growth as an image of spiritual fruitfulness (see Mark 4.1–20 and parallels; Gal. 5.19–26). The writer of Hebrews' concern is solely with his readers' lack of growth in faith. Exceptionally, he is not concerned with the literal meaning of the Old Testament text (any more than Paul in I Cor. 9.9), so there is no basis here for arguing that when crops fail in developing countries, it is a sign of God's displeasure.

6.9–12   The writer at last returns from strenuous warning to encouragement. God's *people* is literally 'the holy ones', here not angels but Christians. Service to God's people is evidence of *love of* God's *name*, that is, of God himself (compare Matt. 25.31–46). The readers, too, are no doubt members of God's people. 6.10 probably refers to service of those members of the Christian community, for example, those imprisoned for their faith, who are in special need (see 13.1ff.; 10.32ff.). 6.11 is an emphatic concluding appeal to *each one* of the readers. *Keenness* is related to the verb translated 'make every effort' in 4.11; it is the opposite of the readers' sluggishness and laxity (5.11; 6.12). Once more (compare 3.6, 14), the writer expresses his concern that the readers should hold on to their faith *to the end*. This leads him to introduce another argument from the Old Testament, this time based on the *patience* (better 'perseverance', NJB, or 'endurance') of Abraham. Yet the underlying direction in which the argument is moving is not backward but forward: what matters, as in chapter 11, is the believers' *hope* (6.11), and the *inheritance* (6.12; cf. 1.3) which God has promised them.

6.13–20   *God's sure promise*

The point of this passage becomes clear only when it is seen as part of the wider sweep of Hebrews. The last few chapters, despite words of encouragement from time to time, may have proved on the whole disturbing to a community tending to become set in its ways. Chapters 3 and 4 brought a call to listen with fresh attentiveness to God's voice, and a warning about failing to enter his place of rest. The first part of ch. 6 had reinforced the warning in the sternest terms yet. Now the writer returns to the more positive side of his message. In ch. 2 he had spoken warmly about the close links between Jesus and those who become related to him by membership of God's family or people. Underlying the warnings of 3.7–4.11 was the positive theme that God's place of rest was still available, still open to those who remained faithful to the end.

Now the writer repeats this message in different language. In Gen. 22.17, he says, God made to Abraham the solemn promise of an 'inheritance' (6.12), that is, for Hebrews, a land to possess. This is not in fact the main point of the Genesis passage, which rather stresses Abraham's countless descendants, his victories over his enemies, and his future role as the one through whom 'all nations on earth will wish to be blessed' (Gen. 22.18). Similarly Ecclus. (Ben Sira) 44.19ff. calls Abraham 'the great father of a host of nations'; he was promised that 'his family should be countless as the dust of the earth, and . . . that their territories should extend from sea to sea'. True, these passages also emphasize, in the spirit of Heb. 6.12, Abraham's obedience to God, expressed in his willingness to sacrifice his son Isaac. 'When put to the test he proved steadfast' (Ecclus. 44.20). But the writer of Hebrews is not interested in human descendants, 'a host of nations', an earthly promised land, or the victories of God's people over their enemies. More precisely, he is interested in such matters only as 'types' pointing forward to a better, heavenly land which God has promised to his people, if they remain faithful. The same God who promised the land of Israel to Abraham, and kept his promise, will surely keep the greater promise to his people which remains outstanding. The call for the readers to remain faithful to God is now outweighed by the assurance of God's faithfulness to his people. For it is one people, under both the old order and the new.

In this passage, even the distinction between the old and new promises, the earthly and the heavenly 'inheritance', is not stressed; but vv. 19f. point clearly towards heaven.

6.13   God made his promise to Abraham doubly secure by combining it with a vow or oath. Modern English is poorer than Greek and some other languages in two ways. First, it has no verb related to 'vow' or 'oath' meaning 'to swear'; and second, 'swear' is often used of cursing or other bad language, which is irrelevant here. Most cultures have traditions of swearing oaths, and calling down supernatural punishments if an oath is not kept. In Israel belief in a single God made an oath sworn by him, or by his name, especially binding (see for example Gen. 21.23; 24.3; Ex. 22.11; Josh. 2.12; I Sam. 24.21; II Sam. 19.7; Jer. 4.2). Jesus' command 'not to swear at all' (Matt. 5.33–37; compare 23.16–22; Lev. 19.12; Num. 30.2; Deut. 23.21) was one of the points at which Jesus radically deepened and transformed the traditional understanding of the law of Moses.

If then it is so solemn a matter for a human being to call God to witness to the truth of what one says, how much more solemn a matter must it be for God himself, whose simple promise would surely be enough, to deign to confirm it by an oath, as he did to Abraham (see also Jer. 22.5 for God 'swearing by himself').

The writer's preoccupation with status, already shown in ch. 1, and shortly to reappear in 7.7, reappears here. He expects his readers to assume as something beyond discussion that oaths are sworn by someone of higher status than oneself; Jesus, too, argues with the scribes and Pharisees on the basis of this assumption in Matt. 23.16–22. It follows that, since there is no one of higher status than God, God can swear only by himself; and this he does to Abraham.

6.14–15   Again, as in v. 12, the writer emphasizes Abraham's patience or endurance. He had obeyed God, even to the point of being willing to put to death his son Isaac, the basis, humanly speaking, of all his hopes of the posterity which God had promised.

When Hebrews uses the word *promise*, it is always good to ask whether it means (1) the promise itself, the act of promising, or (2) what is promised, the content of the promise. Here it could be either or both, because the quotation from Gen. 22.17 is indeed an emphatic promise (literally, using a common Hebraic form, 'blessing I will bless you and multiplying I will multiply you'; compare Luke 22.15, 'with desire I have desired'). GNB, NIV and NJB all choose (2). GNB has 'he received what God had promised', pointing back to the earlier promises in Gen. 17.2; 18.10. This is possible, but the writer of Hebrews has the Gen. 22 passage primarily in mind, so 'received what was promised' (NIV) is probably better.

6.16–20 form a single sentence in Greek; one in which there is some repetition for rhetorical effect. In v. 16, as in 9.16f., the writer appeals, not to Scripture, but to current practice in the society to which he and the readers belong. *Sets a limit to what can be called in question* is a careful translation of the Greek words, which may, however, mean no more than 'puts an end to all argument' (NIV). In v. 17, *the heirs of his promise* means 'those who were to receive what he promised' (GNB). 'How immutable' (v. 17) and 'irrevocable' (v. 18) are closely related in Greek: literally 'the immutability . . . immutable'.

The *two irrevocable acts* in v. 18 are the promise and the oath; a distinction probably more important to the first readers than to most Westerners today. In the background is the requirement of Deut. 17.2–6, referred to in Heb. 10.28, for evidence from at least two witnesses who agreed. *God could not possibly play us false* is literally 'impossible [compare 6.4] for God to lie' – that is, directly, to Abraham. But the writer's concern is rapidly moving away from the Old Testament to 'us', as the next sentence makes explicit. *Laid claim* is a doubtful translation of an unusual word which other versions translate literally as 'fled'. The word is used in Acts 14.6 of Paul and Barnabas fleeing from one city to another. The 'promise' to Abraham is now transformed into a *hope set before us*; it is the hope of 'inheriting', that is, of being given by God, a better 'land' than Israel. At the same time, the basis for the hope moves from the promise and oath which God made to Abraham, to the journey from earth to heaven which Jesus has made on our behalf as our high priest. Grammatically, what is said to be *safe and secure*, and to *enter . . . the sanctuary behind the curtain* may be either (1) the 'hope', or (2) the 'anchor' with which it is compared. NJB prefers (2), and other versions leave the question open. The picture language is clearer if (1) is chosen, so that the metaphor of the anchor is not pressed too far.

The image of the *curtain* (6.19) between the outer and the inner sanctuaries of the Temple will be fully discussed in chapter 9. Here the idea is sown and left in the readers' mind, as the idea of Jesus as high priest was first sown in 2.17. 'Forerunner' means essentially the same as 'pioneer' in 2.10; 12.2. The chapter ends with another reminder of Ps. 110.4, first quoted in 5.6.

7.1–28   *A high priest like Melchizedek*

The time has now come, after three preliminary mentions of Melchizedek (5.6, 10; 6.20) to discuss this mysterious figure in detail. The writer works back from Ps. 110.4 to the only other mention of Melchizedek in the Bible, in Gen. 14.17–20. This chapter is quite mysterious in itself. It does not fit neatly into its context or into the sources into which scholars divide most of the Pentateuch. It mentions quite a number of people and places which are difficult to identify, and which are not mentioned elsewhere in the Bible. It is likely that the writer of Hebrews found it significant that Melchizedek is the first priest mentioned in the Bible. His authority thus owes nothing to Aaron, Levi, or Moses, all of whom came much later.

It is also likely, though not provable, that the writer of Hebrews was aware of currents of speculation about Melchizedek, strong traces of which have been found in the Dead Sea Scrolls. A document found in Cave XI at Qumran depicts him as presiding over a heavenly court of justice. There is more about Melchizedek in I Enoch, probably written before Hebrews, and in II Enoch, probably written just after Hebrews. Speculation about him continued into the Middle Ages. The writer of Hebrews is more cautious than these writers, and bases himself primarily on the biblical texts and on what can be deduced from them by the kind of arguments used by ancient Jewish scholars.

The importance of Melchizedek for Hebrews should not be exaggerated. His main concern is with the high priesthood of Christ, to which Ps. 110.4 points. Since this verse mentions Melchizedek, discussion of Melchizedek himself is a necessary step towards understanding what it means to say that Christ is a high priest 'like Melchizedek'. But direct discussion of Melchizedek is confined to Heb. 7.1–10; in vv. 11–19, he is referred to only in the set phrase 'like' or 'in the order of Melchizedek'; and in vv. 20–28, he is not mentioned at all, attention being concentrated exclusively on Jesus as high priest.

The language of vv. 1ff., though based on Gen. 14.17–20, contains rhythmic, even poetic elements (though what 'poetic' means in a New Testament setting is difficult to define). Various attempts have been made to find within these verses a hymn about Melchizedek, one perhaps Jewish rather than Christian in origin. Such attempts are interesting but inconclusive. It remains probable that the argument in

vv. 1–10, though based primarily on the biblical texts, is influenced (especially in v. 3) by the writer's awareness of contemporary interest in this obscure figure.

7.1f. condense the Genesis passage and add an explanation of the name Melchizedek which is generally accurate. The writer of Hebrews omits the reference in Gen. 14.18 to Melchizedek bringing food and wine to Abraham. This would have blurred the argument by suggesting that, in one respect, Melchizedek served Abraham. (No New Testament writer, incidentally, uses the form 'Abram', used in Gen. 14.) The total effect of these verses is to emphasize Melchizedek's high status. The implication, which will be drawn out at length in vv. 4–10, is that he is superior even to Abraham.

7.3 advances the argument with the help of a rabbinic assumption that, since Scripture contains all truth, anything not stated in Scripture may be assumed not to be the case. Rabbis had a saying: 'What is not in Torah [the law of Moses] is not in the world.' This argument is of course used selectively. The writer of Hebrews uses it to show that, since Gen. 14 (not to mention Ps. 110.4) says nothing either of Melchizedek's parents nor of his other ancestors, he did not have any. Moreover, more directly important for the argument about priesthood, since the Bible does not mention either his birth or his death, he neither was born nor died. The writer skilfully sidesteps the irrelevant question of Melchizedek's birth (which II Enoch 71, on the contrary, describes in imaginative detail). There is no reference here to the virgin birth of Jesus. The fact that Melchizedek did not die is, however, significant; it means that he 'remains a priest for all time'. This is yet another allusion to Ps. 110.4, though the wording is slightly different. This in turn means that Melchizedek bears *the likeness of the Son of God* (literally, 'having been made like the Son of God'). This is the converse of the psalm's reference to 'a priest for ever, like Melchizedek'.

The writer has thus virtually reached the position of proving that Jesus is the eternal priest of which the psalm speaks. He is thus almost ready to throw away the Melchizedekian ladder by which he has climbed to this conclusion, which later verses will amplify. The phrase 'bearing the likeness of the Son of God' remains puzzling. Normally in Hebrews we know whether other beings, such as the angels, Moses, and Old Testament priests, are contrasted with the Son as his inferiors (as in ch. 1; 3.1–6; and ch. 9), or whether Old Testament figures are being quoted simply as good or bad examples, as in ch. 11 and 3.7–4.11 respectively. With Melchizedek, we are not sure. One scholar has repeatedly urged that the writer of Hebrews really thought that Melchizedek was Jesus in a pre-incarnate form, but that he did not quite have the courage to say so. This is tempting but unlikely. It is more probable, though still unprovable, that the writer is in effect saying to his readers: 'We know there is a lot of speculation going on about this mysterious priest. If you study carefully what the Bible says about him, it will point you to Jesus, our great high priest.'

7.4   The writer now leaves detailed comments on the Genesis text, and moves on to more far-reaching exposition. The word translated 'the finest of the spoil' or 'the finest plunder' (NJB) may simply mean 'the plunder' (NIV, similarly NRSV, GNB). In the Greek, the word 'patriarch' comes at the end of the sentence, giving it added weight.

7.5, 9f.   But Melchizedek is not merely an individual who on a particular occasion showed the he had higher status than Abraham. He is the representative of a different and higher kind of priesthood than that exercised by the descendants of Abraham through Levi and Aaron. These verses spell the contrast out as follows.

(1) In principle, every male member of the Aaronic branch of the tribe of Levi automatically became a priest. In practice, certain physical handicaps disqualified one from becoming a priest, but descent from Aaron was a *sine qua non*. Such priests were not only permitted but required by the Mosaic law (Num. 18.21) to tithe their fellow-Israelites, even though they are all, priests and laymen, descendants of Abraham. So the implied order of precedence runs:

> Abraham
> priests
> Levites
> laymen.

(Women and children do not come into this discussion.)

(2) The story of Melchizedek points to the existence of an independent and radically different hierarchy:

> Melchizedek
> Abraham
> Abraham's descendants (see vv. 9–10).

The rest of the passage, including *vv. 7–8*, fills in details of the argument. (a) Melchizedek's high status is seen still more clearly when it is remembered that Abraham was the one to whom God had made the promises (doubtless those discussed in 6.13–18). (b) Melchizedek's superiority to Abraham is seen not only by his tithing Abraham, but by his blessing him (Gen. 14.19–20; the blessing mentioned in Heb. 7.2 is not quoted). (c) It is a basic principle *beyond all dispute* (in technical terms, axiomatic) that it is always the superior who blesses the inferior (v. 7). (Texts like Ps. 135.19f.; 145.1–2, 10, 21, in which human worshippers *bless the Lord*, are only apparent exceptions, since *bless* in such contexts means 'praise'.) (d) The levitical priests are mortal; Melchizedek is immortal, as v. 3 proved from the fact that Scripture says nothing about his death (v. 8). (e) In a manner of speaking, what Abraham did in subordinating himself to Melchizedek, potentially involved his descendants, including Levi and all *his* priestly descendants. This means that the two hierarchies diagrammed above are not only contrasted (like Paul's *in Adam . . . in Christ*, I Cor. 15.22): the second is subordinated to the first, Melchizedek taking his place above Abraham. Whoever Melchizedek is (and the writer never identifies him clearly), he is so important that any priest described as 'like Melchizedek' must be far superior to any levitical priest. The nature of that superiority will now be explored in greater detail.

7.11–19 form a passage of concentrated logical argument: the word translated *for* in vv. 13 and 17, and *since* in v. 19, in fact occurs seven times in these verses. This and following passages tend to be difficult for the modern reader. One reason for this is that the writer works with different presuppositions (see especially v. 12). Another is that, as in many non-Western traditions, the argument moves not in a straight line, but round the subject, approaching it now from one side, now from another. Within its own terms, however, the passage is carefully ordered and deserves to be taken seriously. It may be helpful to read first verses such as 7.26 and 8.1, where the writer states the *main point* up to which he has been leading. We can usually accept his conclusions as expressing the heart of Christianity, even if the route by which he led his first readers there remains at times obscure for us.

7.11 opens the theme, and v. 19 will seal it: that theme is *perfection*, and how to attain it. *Perfection* is a many-sided word. In Hebrews, it is best approached in the setting of worship, seen as the means of approach to God. Now worship, for the writer of Hebrews, involves sacrifice; and a sacrifice, under the Old Testament law, had to be 'perfect', in the sense of having 'no defect in it. You are to present to the LORD nothing blind, disabled, mutilated, with a running sore, scab, or eruption . . .' (Lev. 22.21f.). By extension, the law itself was said to be *perfect*, in the sense of being a complete and undistorted expression of God's will (Ps. 19.7; compare 18.30; II Sam. 22.31, which speaks similarly of God's *way*). Applied to human beings, perfection, especially in Hebrews, becomes a process by which God's will is completely worked out, whether in Jesus through his suffering (2.10; compare 7.28); or in those who are consecrated by his offering of himself (10.1, 14; compare 9.9; 11.40; 12.23). Perfection is therefore more than the absence of sin. Nevertheless, before God's purpose for the believer can be fulfilled: that is, before the believer can enjoy uninterrupted access to God in worship, sin has to be 'covered' or blotted out and the conscience cleansed.

The writer of Hebrews sees the Old Testament system of priesthood and sacrifice as having been set up by God to accomplish this purpose. Never does he question that this system was of divine institution. There is no reason to think that this is just a matter of tact; the writer himself, together with his Jewish readers, believes it. He is as sincere about this as Paul is when he insists that the law is 'holy, spiritual and good' (Rom. 7.12, 14, 16; compare I Tim. 1.8). The only difference is that whereas Paul is most interested in the moral law, the writer of Hebrews is concerned with the law as setting out in detail God's requirements for worship. If the Old Testament system has failed, the fault is not God's but mankind's. For Old Testament prophets such as Jeremiah, the fault is specifically Israel's; but Hebrews never mentions Israel outside the quotation in 8.8, 10).

The language of v. 11 is a little tortuous, since it involves an unreal condition and a rhetorical question. If these are removed, the meaning is: 'There was no perfect sacrifice, and therefore no unimpeded access to God, through the levitical priesthood. So another kind of priest was needed, one like Melchizedek.' The words which REB puts in brackets probably do not merely mean that the Old Testament law contained regulations about the priesthood. Nor do they mean that the priests themselves gave the law, though in fact both Hilkiah the high priest and other priests played an important part in the recovery of the law under Josiah (II Kings 22–23; II Chron. 34). They mean, as REB says, that the priesthood was fundamental to the law, and thus to the people of Israel as a whole.

The word for *another kind* is the word translated *new* in v. 15, where it is emphatic. The point is that the Melchizedekian priesthood is not just *another* priesthood alongside that of Levi through Aaron: it is different in kind. The words are, however, literally 'a different high priest'; the reference is exclusively to Jesus.

7.12   like the end of 9.22, states something which the writer assumes his readers will accept without question. He does not say, as we might expect, 'a change in the law entails a change of priesthood'; he says the converse. The general principle involved is that priesthood is more fundamental than the law. But deeper even than the general principle is the fact of what God has done through Christ. God has in fact set up a new kind of priesthood (8.1), thus relativizing everything the old law said about priesthood and worship. *Must*, literally 'of necessity', is a logical expression: 'a change of law necessarily follows'.

7.13f.   follow up more specifically the appeal to history. *He who is spoken of here* is the 'other' or 'different priest' of v. 11. The writer has almost completed the gentle transition from Melchizedek to Jesus, though Jesus is not named until v. 22, or called *high priest* again until 7.26. Melchizedek has no ancestry (v. 3), whereas it is a matter of public record that Jesus was a descendant of Judah (see Matt. 1.2; Luke 3.33), a tribe to which the Mosaic law (perhaps especially Deut. 33.7–11) does not assign any priestly function. The word translated *spring* in v. 14, and more literally *arise* in v. 15, may recall what is said in Num. 24.17 about a star which is to *rise* from Jacob; the same verb is used in the Greek of Jer. 23.5, speaking of a descendant of David who would rule Israel wisely.

7.15ff.   But the argument does not depend primarily on the facts of physical descent. Indeed a fundamental point here, expressed in different ways in other parts of the New Testament also, is that membership of God's people does not depend on physical descent (compare Matt. 3.9 and parallel; John 8.33–58; Rom. 9–11; Gal. 4.21–31). This is something which most Christians tend to take for granted, but the preoccupation of New Testament writers with this theme shows how radically new it was for a church born out of Judaism. The interest taken in it by the writer of Hebrews is all the more remarkable since he is not concerned with the mission to Gentiles. On *has arisen* in v. 15, see comment on v. 14.

In 7.16   the writer moves a step further from form to substance. This new kind of priest has not only higher status than the old (see vv. 4–10), but also greater power. This point will be expanded in vv. 23f.

For the moment, the writer refers on the one hand to the words 'for ever' in Ps. 110–14 (quoted again in 7.17 to clinch the argument), and perhaps on the other hand to what Christians already believe (compare 13.20) about the resurrection of Jesus. By contrast, the system of rules in the old law (literally, 'law of commandment'), on which the old priesthood was based, was literally 'fleshly'. This word probably means, not the opposite of 'spiritual', as in Rom. 7.14 and I Cor. 3.1, but 'relating to descent' (similarly RSV, NIV, NJB). Not far from the writer's thought, however, is the fact that anything 'fleshly' is weak and ineffective (v. 18), lacking *the power of a life that cannot be destroyed*. So GNB's translation 'human', though perhaps too general, points in the right direction.

Verses 7.18–19   sum up this stage of the argument in the form of a contrast, basically: 'the earlier commandment is repealed: a hope of something better is introduced.' The following details may be noted: (1) the word translated *rules*, here and in v. 15, is in fact singular; in this passage, the distinction between 'law' and 'commandment' is somewhat blurred. (2) The reason for the repeal of the old command- ment or law is stated twice: (a) it was *ineffective and useless*. (The Greek work for *useless* is, as it happens, the name given to the 'anopheles' mosquito, which carries the malarial parasite; but here the word means 'useless', not 'harmful'; in Titus 3.9 it is translated 'unprofit- able'.) (b) More specifically, *the law perfected nothing*; see comment on v. 11. *Nothing* essentially means 'no one'; it is just possible that there is a side glance at animal sacrifices under the old order. (3) *Hope* of something (less probably 'someone') *better* does not refer to a vague future possibility. *Hope*, here as elsewhere in Hebrews (see 3.6) and the rest of the New Testament, is firmly rooted in God's promises, as is shown by the quotation in v. 17, and the reference to God's *oath* in v. 20. (4) *Through which* must grammatically mean 'through which hope'; but underlying the grammar, the writer is pointing to Christ as the content of that hope. (5) To *draw near to God* is the purpose of worship; elsewhere (e.g. 4.16) the writer uses a different verb for 'approaching' God, but the meaning is the same. It is the fulfilment of the purpose indicated by Hebrews' use of the word *perfection*. Paul uses different language, notably 'justification by faith' (GNB 'being put right with God'), to describe the same reality, namely the removal of all barriers between God and humanity. Both ways of speaking have their roots in the Old Testament: Hebrews' in the rules for sacrifice, Paul's in the quasi-legal arguments between God and his people, in such passages as Isa. 43.8–12.

7.20–28 now apply the argument explicitly to Jesus: Melchizedek has served his purpose; his status has been explained in the light of what God has done in Christ.

7.20ff. form a single sentence in Greek, which REB extensively and successfully restructures. GNB keeps closer to the original order, but divides the sentence into four. For an idea of the complexity of the original sentence structure, see AV. Verses 20–21 appear on first reading to take a step back to the discussion of oaths in 6.13–20, but in fact they introduce the only quotation of the opening words of Ps. 110.4: *The Lord has sworn and will not go back on his word*. The argument in 6.13–20 is now presupposed, and not repeated. God swore no oath in establishing the old priesthood; but he did swear an oath in appointing Jesus to his new kind of priesthood. The writer cuts the quotation short for two reasons: (1) because further reference to Melchizedek would now be a step back, and (2) because the words 'for ever' attest an essential aspect of the newness and superiority of Christ's priesthood: he remains perpetually in office. This theme will be explored in vv. 22–25.

7.22 stands alongside 2.17 and 5.6f. as one of the key verses of Hebrews. Indeed, it is a verse which links Hebrews with other strands in the New Testament and announces the theme of the 'new covenant' which gives the New Testament its name. 'Testament' comes from the Latin translation of a Greek word which means both 'covenant', as usually in Hebrews, and 'will', as in 9.16f. A covenant is basically an agreement or treaty, either between individuals or between groups of people. For many centuries, in the ancient Near East, it was common for a less powerful ruler or vassal to put himself under the protection of a more powerful ruler or suzerain by means of a covenant. In such an agreement the conditions were largely laid down by the suzerain who promised support in return for the vassal's loyalty. In the Bible, God takes the part of the suzerain, and unilaterally grants a covenant to his people, who promise to be faithful. The terms of the covenant may be summed up in God saying, first to Israel and later to the church: You will be my people, and I shall be your God (Ex. 25.8; 29.45; Lev. 26.12; Jer. 31.1; Ezek. 37.27; II Cor. 6.16; Rev. 21.3). The terms of the new covenant prophesied by Jeremiah (see Heb. 8.8–12) are the same as those of the old. It is not a completely different type of covenant (as Christ's high priesthood is different in kind from the levitical), but a re-founding of the old covenant on a fresh basis, namely that of personal knowledge of and loyalty to God. This second foundation has become necessary because God's people has not kept the conditions of the first covenant. Jesus links the establishment of the new covenant with his death: it is 'the new covenant sealed by my blood' (Luke 22.20, REB margin; I Cor. 11.26; compare Mark 14.24; Matt. 26.28; Matthew and Mark do not have the word 'new').

It is clear that the theme of the new covenant is important in Hebrews; it is more difficult to say exactly how important. This is, perhaps surprisingly, the first mention of a covenant in Hebrews. The fullest discussion of the theme will come in 9.1–23, where the new covenant is contrasted with the 'old' or 'first' covenant. This discussion is introduced by the quotation of Jer. 31.31–34 in Heb. 8.8–12 – the longest quotation in the New Testament, partly repeated in 10.16f. In both places the writer of Hebrews largely leaves the quotation to speak for itself. In 9.20 the writer refers to the establishment of God's first covenant with his people, quoting Ex. 24.8. The language of that passage suggests that the writer of Hebrews is aware of the tradition that Jesus, at the Last Supper, spoke of a new covenant in his blood. In later chapters there are only two passing references to the 'new' or 'eternal' covenant, in 12.24 and 13.20 respectively.

The evidence thus suggests that the theme of the new covenant was, for the writer of Hebrews, an important way of expressing the superiority of the new order, with its different form of priesthood and sacrifice. He knew that he was building on and developing earlier Christian tradition, handed down as coming ultimately from Jesus himself, rather than striking out in a fresh direction as he does in his teaching about Jesus as high priest.

This new covenant is *the covenant which Jesus guarantees*. The word translated *guarantees* is not used elsewhere in the Greek Bible, nor is any word related to it. In secular Greek it refers to someone who gives security, primarily in a business deal, but also (as here) in a treaty. For the writer of Hebrews it is another way of stressing for his readers the absolute security of God's new covenant, as something on which they may utterly rely. *Jesus*, as usual, is emphatic.

7.23ff.   express another contrast between the old and new covenants and draw a positive conclusion. It was natural for a people which believed in one God to assume that a single figure was better than a number of individuals. In particular a high priest who holds office *for ever* (Ps. 110.4, repeated in v. 24) was better than a number of high priests (83, according to the Jewish historian Josephus, from Aaron to the destruction of the Temple in 70 CE) who die and therefore have to be replaced. The word in v. 24 translated 'perpetual' is sometimes understood to mean that Christ's high priesthood 'does not pass on to someone else' (GNB), but this meaning is not attested.

The conclusion is that a perpetual priest, that is, by implication, Jesus alone, can *save completely those who approach God through him.* *Save* overlaps considerably in meaning with *brought . . . to perfection* in v. 19, and *approach* means the same as *draw near*, also in v. 19. The new step forward is the statement of what Christ does now in heaven. He pleads on behalf of believers, as he is said in Rom. 8.34 to do 'at God's right hand' (compare *raised high above the heavens* in Heb. 7.26; see also I John 2.1). A stronger form of the same verb is used in Rom. 8.26 of the Holy Spirit 'pleading for us'. This is a strain of common Christian tradition which the writer of Hebrews accepts but does not emphasize, perhaps because he wishes rather to stress the effectiveness of Christ's one self-offering in death. The statement of Ps. 110.4 about his being a priest *for ever* is transmuted in vv. 24–25 into a statement about the power of his indestructible life.

7.26ff. is a hymn of praise to Christ which recalls the praise of Melchizedek at the beginning of the chapter. *Such a high priest* does not imply that there is any other candidate for the post than Jesus (compare 'a Son' in 1.2). The words introduce, without naming him, a description of Jesus as high priest which fill out the picture already sketched in 2.17 and 4.15f. *Suited to our need* is the verb translated *it was fitting* in 2.10. In neither place is the writer speculating, but rather describing and giving inward assent to what God has done in Christ.

All but the last item in the description in v. 26 is language appropriate to a perfect sacrifice (in the terms of Num. 18.21, alluded to in v. 5). The word for *holy*, not used elsewhere in Hebrews, is applied to Jesus as God's 'holy one' in Acts 2.27; 13.35 (both quoting Ps. 16.10; REB 'your faithful servant'); also to God in Rev. 15.4; 16.5. *Innocent* is not used elsewhere in the New Testament of Jesus. It is a general word meaning simply the opposite of evil. In Proverbs (e.g. 1.4), as in Rom. 16.18, it is used of 'simple' people. *Undefiled* suggests physical purity, as in 13.10 and Wisdom 3.13; 8.20, and by extension spiritual purity, as in James 1.27 of pure religion, I Peter 1.4 of believers' inheritance 'which nothing can . . . spoil,' and especially in the present verse of Jesus himself. He is *set apart from sinners*, untouched by their sin (4.15): this is the negative counterpart of being *holy* and therefore set apart for God's service. *Raised high above the heavens* anchors the writer's teaching about Christ's high priesthood in the traditional teaching (1.3). For the plural *heavens* see comment on 4.14.

So far this passage has seemed like a summing up or a resonant conclusion. Verses 27f. also contain some repetition of earlier ideas: the *weakness* of the old high priests and the order they represented, vv. 18, 23; reference to God's *oath* establishing the new priesthood, v. 28, recalling v. 20. The writer typically combines this with an important step forward. He announces in advance a major theme of chapter 9, namely the thought of Jesus as the one effective sacrifice. The word translated *once for all* is one of the writer's favourites. It occurs in Greek in two related forms. The first is used of Christ's sacrifice in 9.26, 27, 28, and of Christians in 6.4; 10.2. The second, possibly more emphatic, form is used of the death of Christ in 7.27; 9.12 and 10.10.

The contrast between Christ and the old priests is pressed home in v. 27. The writer may be fusing the description of the daily sacrifices with the account of the liturgy for the annual Day of Atonement (Lev. 16.6, 15; compare 9.7, 15). There 'Aaron' (later understood to include any of his successors as high priest) is instructed to offer sacrifice, first for himself and his family, and then for the people as a whole. (On the people of God in Hebrews, see comment on 2.17; 4.9.) Christ needs only to offer one sacrifice. Since he is sinless (4.15; 7.26), he needs only to offer sacrifice for the people. The greatest difference is that whereas the old priests offered animal sacrifices (also other forms of offering, which do not interest the writer of Hebrews), Christ *offered up himself* (two emphatic words in the Greek). *He did this* may mean 'he offered sacrifice for the people', or more generally 'he offered sacrifice.' The word for *offered up* earlier included the idea of raising, for example to put a sacrifice up on an altar; but by New Testament times it has become a technical term for offering in sacrifice. Hebrews will use it again in 9.28, of Christ 'bearing' the sins of mankind, and in 13.15, of Christians 'offering' praise.

The first part of v. 28, as already indicated, is largely repetition; so indeed is the second part, but it is remarkable in two ways. First, for the way in which it now applies to the Son the phrase *for ever*, which Ps. 110.4 used of the 'priest like Melchizedek'. Second, for its statement that the Son *has been made perfect*. Even apart from the words *for ever*, the tense of the verb suggests a permanent state; in this case, a completion of Christ's mission which can never be undone.

8.1–13 *The new covenant*

As the last few verses of ch. 7 have just shown, the writer of Hebrews, like a good teacher, combines old and new teaching; what look like summaries usually include a fresh point. This is so here. He begins by identifying the *main point* (NRSV, similarly NJB; 'the point', RSV, NIV; 'the whole point'. GNB) of (literally) 'the things that are being said'. The *high priest . . . suited to our need* (7.26) has in fact come. As the writer has several times recalled, from 1.3. onwards, this high priest has now taken his place at God's right hand. The writer now makes this old teaching the starting-point for an important new development, which will go on into ch. 9. This is the comparison and contrast between the earthly and the heavenly sanctuary, and between the sacrifices which are offered in each.

The writer typically sees the relation between the two from various points of view. (1) The earthly sanctuary and its sacrifices are simply contrasted, the ineffective with the effective (e.g. 9.8). (2) Since every contrast presupposes a basis for comparison, the writer points to features which the two sanctuaries and their sacrifices have in common (e.g. 8.3; 9.21f.). (3) The old covenant is seen as pointing towards its fulfilment in the new, as in 9.18–22. (4) The two covenants are used in a 'how much more' type of argument (see comment on 2.1ff.), as in 9.23. (5) The picture of the earthly and heavenly sanctuaries allows the writer to describe the relation between Christ's death once for all on earth, and his continuing ministry (see 7.25) in heaven.

Once again, this teaching was calculated to encourage the readers by reminding them of what they already knew and believed, but then lead them on to new teaching. The quotation of Jer. 31.31–34 says to the readers in effect: 'As you see, even the new covenant is spoken of in the old Scriptures which you know and recognize as holy.' This interweaving of old and new is not just good teaching method. It was essential to the writer's purpose, since he was convinced (see 6.4ff.) that his readers must go forward, if they were not to fall back and be lost.

8.1 *Majesty* is a reverent way of speaking about God, as REB made explicit in 1.3. The Jews refused and still refuse to pronounce God's proper name, Yahweh, and have various ways of speaking of him indirectly. Some of this reticence remains in Hebrews, in speaking both of God and of Jesus (see comment on 2.9).

8.2   The word for *minister*, used also in 1.7. may be used of one human being who serves another (as Paul uses the word of Epaphroditus in Phil. 2.25), or of someone carrying out a public service. More commonly it is used of someone who serves God (Rom. 13.6) or Christ (15.16). Here it means someone who serves God by leading a service of worship.

The *real sanctuary*, as the previous verse has shown, is heaven. There is a strong current of Greek thought, going back at least to the philosopher Plato (427–347 BCE), and extending well into the Christian era, which holds that the world perceived by the senses is only a reflection of the 'ideal', that is the 'real' world. It is probable that the writer of Hebrews had met this type of thinking in a popularized form (see especially 8.5; 10.1). There is no evidence that he read Plato for himself, and there is disagreement about whether he had read any of the works of the Jewish Platonist Philo (about 20 BCE to about 50 CE). In particular Plato's rather static contrast between the two worlds is less important for the writer of Hebrews than his dynamic view of the action of God in history, which dominates almost all parts of the Bible (Ecclesiastes is generally an exception). What Hebrews says here about the *real sanctuary* recalls, however, what John says, using the same word, about Jesus as the 'true (or real) light' (1.9); about God giving 'the true bread from heaven' (6.32); and about Jesus as 'the true vine' (15.1).

The *tent* was originally just that: a small, portable sanctuary, sometimes called 'the tabernacle', carried by the Israelites during their wanderings after the exodus from Egypt. A detailed description of how it was to be built, and then of how it was in fact built, is given in Ex. 25–30 and 35–40 respectively. This description probably includes many features drawn from the later permanent sanctuary in Solomon's Temple. An older description of a simple type of shrine, called the 'Tent of Meeting', is found in Ex. 33.7–11. There is no evidence that the writer of Hebrews distinguished between the two. What he says about the sanctuary, notably in 9.1–7, is based on the Exodus accounts rather than on anything in the Second Temple, built by Herod, which was probably still standing when Hebrews was written. In the present passage, the writer speaks of the sanctuary as a whole. It is probably only in 9.2f. that he distinguishes between its outer and inner parts (but see also the comment on 9.6f.).

The second part of v. 2 recalls the Greek of Num. 24.6, which speaks of 'tents which the Lord pitched'. The writer of Hebrews takes this to mean that they were set up by no human hand.

8.3 The function of a high priest is to offer sacrifices; this principle must therefore also apply to Jesus (*this one*). The writer has already stated (7.27) in what Jesus' sacrifice consists; he will discuss the matter again in 9.26, and especially in 10.5–10. *Gifts and sacrifices*, as in 5.1, is a set phrase to cover cereal and animal offerings, but the writer of Hebrews shows no interest in the former.

8.4 Now he builds on his previous teaching about Melchizedek, and on the common belief in Christ's exaltation, to show how Christ's ministry differs from that of the levitical priests. An unreal condition (compare 7.11), *if he were on earth* (which now he is not), is contrasted with what is *in fact* (v. 6) the case. Jesus could not have been a priest during his earthly life. The reason for this is not only (as was argued in 7.14), because he belonged to the wrong tribe, but also because, so to speak, there are no vacancies in the earthly priesthood. On that level, priests and sacrifices have been provided for in the law.

8.5 But these are not the real priest or the real sacrifice. Their *sanctuary . . . is only a shadowy symbol*, literally, 'copy and shadow of', perhaps 'preliminary sketch for', *the heavenly one* (compare 10.1). This argument is supported by a quotation from Ex. 25.40 (compare 25.9), and runs implicitly as follows: Moses on Mount Sinai was shown a vision of a heavenly sanctuary, and told to copy it. He did so, as God had told him, as precisely as possible; but a copy, however good an imitation it may be, will always be inferior to the original. Worship under the old order (ignoring any differences between the wilderness tabernacle, Solomon's Temple, and Herod's Temple) is carried on in this imitation tabernacle. But Jesus now carries on his ministry in the original temple in heaven, which Moses saw and tried to copy. In this way (similarly to 3.1–6), a text which was originally intended to emphasize the importance of the tabernacle, as being an *exact* copy of what Moses saw in heaven, is reinterpreted to show its inferiority, as being *only* a copy. The important word in the quotation is now *pattern*. Some have taken this to mean that Moses was only shown a copy of the heavenly tabernacle, and copied that, but this is unnecessarily complicated. God instructed Moses to take the heavenly tabernacle as a pattern for the earthly one.

8.6   The contrast with Jesus' ministry is now drawn. The word correctly translated *in fact* (NJB 'as it is') also means 'now', either in a logical or a temporal sense. *Jesus* is implied. The second half of the verse includes a 'how much more' argument, simplified in most modern translations; more literally '. . . a ministry which is as much more excellent than the old as the covenant he mediates is better, since it is enacted on better promises' (RSV).

Jesus' relation to the new covenant is defined as being that of a 'mediator' (compare 9.15; 12.24; also Gal. 3.19f.; I Tim. 2.5). In ancient times pagan gods were often called on as guarantors of agreements; in the Old Testament, priests and prophets, and especially Moses (Ex. 4.15.; 19.3ff.; 20.19), stood between God and the people as mediators. GNB translates: 'the covenant which [Jesus] arranged between God and his people'. The meaning is close to the description of Jesus as the one who *guarantees* the new covenant (7.22). More importantly, it is also close to the function of a priest as one who mediates between God and a human community.

The word translated *better* also means 'greater'. *Established* is the word used in 7.11 of the giving of the law, and the writer of Hebrews does not contrast law and promise in the way in which Paul does (though see Gal. 3.21). In the present verse the meaning is that the basis of the new covenant is God's promises of something better, namely the new covenant itself (compare Eph. 2.12). The writer now takes for granted his earlier arguments about the utter reliability of anything which God himself guarantees on oath (6.13–20; 7.20ff., 28).

8.7   The institutions of the old covenant go on functioning on their own terms (v. 4). The only problem is that they are ineffective (7.18) because of human sin. So God has superseded them by the sacrifice of Christ, thus making them *obsolete*, so that they *will shortly disappear* (8.13). The writer does not say, here or anywhere else, that the old ritual has actually come to an end.

Faultless is word commonly used of people who are 'blameless', especially Job (e.g. 1.1). However ritually 'perfect' the animal sacrifice under the old covenant might be, the working of the covenant itself was open to God's criticism, because a covenant has two parties, and God's people had not kept its side of the bargain. The covenant has thus broken down. There was no place for Jesus within it (v. 4), but there is a 'place' (the literal meaning of the word translated *occasion*) for the entire old covenant to be replaced by something better.

8.8–13   So God in fact *finds fault* with his people. Jeremiah's words in fact contain more promise than condemnation. The writer may be thinking, not only of the condemnation in the second half of v. 9, but also of II Macc. 2.7, where the same unusual word is used of Jeremiah taking his companions to task, but also looking forward to a time when God would 'finally gather . . . his people together and show . . . them favour'. Hebrews itself keeps the same balance of warning and encouragement.

In the introduction to the quotation, *God* is implied; the implied subject may be 'Scripture', since *the Lord* speaks within the quotation itself.

The writer quotes Jeremiah fairly accurately on the whole (allowing, as always, for the fact that we do not know what Greek Old Testament text, if any, he had before him). Unlike Jeremiah, he uses different words in v. 9 for God 'making' the old covenant from the word used in v. 10 of his 'making' the new; but REB and other translations do not distinguish between them. The word for *write* in v. 10 is stronger than that used in most Greek Old Testament manuscripts; it may be chosen to suggest the permanence of the inscription.

For the rest, the text is allowed to speak for itself. Apart from the key phrase *new covenant*, even the language of Jeremiah does not significantly influence the rest of Hebrews. His brief comment in v. 13 brings out the significance for his argument of the word *new*. The setting up of a new covenant defines the existing covenant as *old*, therefore about to *disappear*. The immediate moral drawn from the quotation is thus negative, related to the old covenant; ch. 9 will begin in the same strain. But the author will draw from the same passage a more hopeful message when he comes to quote it again in 10.16f.

9.1–22   *Earthly and heavenly worship*

The four paragraphs of this section offer (1) a general description of the earthly tabernacle and its contents (vv. 1–5); (2) description of the liturgy which was celebrated there, its significance and its limitations (vv. 6–10); (3) a contrasting positive description of Christ's sacrifice, and what it has achieved (vv. 11–14); and (4) a statement of the necessity for Christ's death.

Throughout the section run three continuous threads: (1) the comparison and contrast between the old order and the new; (2) the sustained effort to understand the relation between the old and the new in terms of worship (rather than, as usually in Paul, in legal or ethical terms); and (3) a to and fro movement between Scripture and the fact of Christ, that is, between God's action in past and present (compare 1.1f.).

This section raises the interesting question of whether the writer thinks of the old covenant and its liturgy as past or present. On the one hand, the verbs in vv. 1f., *had its ordinances . . . was set up*, are past; similar verbs are supplied in the translation of vv. 3ff. On the other hand, the verbs in vv. 6f., describing the liturgy, are present. These facts may be understood in two main ways. (1) The past verbs refer to the original setting up of the tabernacle, and the present verbs to the way in which it (or its successor, the Temple) was used in the writer's own time. Or (2) the past verbs mean what they say, namely that the old order is past, and the present verbs are 'timeless' or general.

(2) is grammatically possible; (1) is more likely as far as it goes; but for a complete explanation one must turn to the wider context. In v. 9, the writer states plainly that *all this*, more precisely the *outer tent*, *is symbolic, pointing to the present time*, which in turn is contrasted with the *new order* (v. 10). The best (though not the simplest) explanation is therefore that the writer sees the old order as 'finished' in principle; the sacrifice of Christ has shown once for all its total ineffectiveness; but its institutions are still in place. In the writer's own careful words, it *is becoming obsolete and growing old*, and *will shortly disappear* (8.13); the new order is *already in being* (see comment on 9.11). The writer and his readers are living in what has been called 'the overlap of the ages'.

If this picture is correct, it fits, as argued in the introduction to this commentary, a date shortly before the destruction of the Temple in 70 CE. More important, it fits the readers' situation, if we are right in thinking that the readers are mostly Jewish Christians, tempted to undervalue their faith in Christ. The writer knows it is futile to pretend that non-Christian Judaism and its institutions have ceased to exist. He may well believe that what one might call the Jewish fall-back position would spell disaster for his readers; but it is still a real option, a real temptation, otherwise there would be no problem, no need for Hebrews to be written. But the death of Christ has made all the old sacrifices obsolete; to show how this has happened is the task of this and the following sections (to 10.18).

9.1 The general sense of this verse is clear, but a number of details need comment. (1) The word for *covenant* is implied: in fact, one has to go back to 8.6 to find it expressed, but there is no doubt that it is to be understood here.

(2) The word for *ordinances* (GNB 'rules'; NIV 'regulations') is used again in v. 10, but not elsewhere in Hebrews. The word is related to the term for 'righteousness', and commonly used for the requirements of the law, understood as expressions of God's will (see Luke 1.6; Rom. 2.26). Note once again Hebrews' exclusive interest in provisions governing worship. Everything had to be done properly and as God had laid down in detail; in a different way, what Christ has done is also *fitting* (2.10; compare 7.26). The writer draws no conclusions for the regulation of Christian worship; conversely, Paul was not concerned, in I Cor. 14.26–40, to support from Scripture his argument that all should be done 'decently and in order'.

(3) Many manuscripts have: *The first covenant* also *had its ordinances* . . . , thus making it clear that the writer is still concerned with what the old and the new order have in common: the contrasts, as in 3.1–6, will come later.

(4) Some versions separate the two items mentioned by translating 'also' later in the verse: for example, '. . . regulations for worship and also an earthly sanctuary'. This is unnecessary: the writer joins the two things closely together, as in REB ('its' before 'sanctuary' is implied).

(5) What REB excellently translates . . . *but it was an earthly sanctuary* is a single, heavily emphasized word in the Greek, meaning simply 'worldly', that is, 'belonging to this world', not to heaven. See 8.2 for a similar contrast, where GNB translated 'man-made'; this is implied here.

9.2f. Verses 2–5 are a single sentence in Greek. Verses 2f. outline the distinction between the outer and inner parts of the 'tent' (a division which was maintained and developed in the later, permanent temples); vv. 4f. mention some items which according to the writer were kept in the inner sanctuary.

An outer tent is literally 'a tent, the first'. The context makes it clear that it is first in space, that is, the first anyone entered, not first in time. There was no way into the inner sanctuary except through the outer.

Set up is a good attempt to translate a word which, depending on the context, may mean 'build' or 'equip' or both. It is used also in 3.3f. ('founder'); 9.6 (see comment); 11.7 ('build').

A Roman Catholic interpretation, grammatically possible and still not entirely abandoned, links the word 'holy' with 'bread', and sees a reference to the Lord's Supper; but the translation *the Holy Place* is certainly correct.

The items mentioned in v. 2 raise no great problems. The repeated use of *the* suggests that the writer is reminding his readers of things with which they are already familiar. *The lampstand* and *the table* with *the Bread of the Presence* on it are mentioned in the same order in Lev. 24.1–9; see also Ex. 25.23–39. Ex. 25.35 specifies that the table and the lampstand are to be placed outside the veil surrounding the holy of holies. The phrase translated *Bread of the Presence* is literally, in Greek, 'bread of the setting out', as one 'sets out' a meal on a table; in Hebrew, literally 'bread of the face', that is, bread set out in the presence of God. In Ex. 25.30, Moses is commanded to set out permanently on the table two rows of six loaves each made with fine flour. According to I Sam. 21.6, the priest had to place fresh bread on the table every sabbath day; the priests then ate the old loaves in the holy place(Lev. 24.3–9). Jesus refers to David and his men eating these loaves (Mark 2.26 and parallels; I Sam. 21.1–6) as an indication of the limited scope and authority of the law.

9.3   At the entrance to the outer sanctuary there was a *screen* (Ex. 26.36) or 'curtain' (GNB, NIV); the entrance to the inner sanctuary is thus *the second curtain*. The *Most Holy Place* is called in NRSV and older translations 'the Holy of Holies', a literal translation of a Hebrew idiom.

9.4   contains a number of problematical details which taken together suggest that the writer did not have personal experience of what went on in the Temple, and did not follow the Old Testament texts precisely. The verse as a whole means that the Most Holy Place contained (1) a golden incense altar, and (2) the Ark of the Covenant, which itself contained (a) a golden urn holding manna, (b) Aaron's staff, and (c) the tablets of the covenant. There are two main problems for which no completely satisfying explanation has been found. (1) Although the writer appears to refer to the incense altar, he uses a word which more commonly means 'incense burner'. He may have been thinking of the rebellion of Korah and his friends (see Num. 16). (2) The incense altar was in fact placed in the outer sanctuary (Ex. 30.1–6). The writer of Hebrews may have misunderstood Ex. 30.6 to mean that the altar was 'over against' the inner side of the curtain dividing the two parts of the sanctuary. Such matters (there are other minor discrepancies) are not likely to trouble Christian preachers and teachers or their hearers today, unless they have a particularly inflexible view of the inspiration of the Bible. Indeed, the evidence suggests that these and similar details did not concern the writer of Hebrews (compare 2.6). Similarly, his statement that the Ark of the Covenant was *plated all over with gold* goes beyond what is said in Ex. 30.3. The writer's main concern is to show that the earthly sanctuary, for all its holiness, and its precious historical associations, has now been superseded by the sacrifice of Christ. For the pot of manna, see Ex. 16.33; for Aaron's staff, see Num. 17.8ff.; and for the tablets of the covenant, on which the ten commandments were inscribed, see Deut. 10.3ff.; compare Ex. 25.16.

9.5 *The cherubim of God's glory* (GNB 'the winged creatures representing God's presence') are the beaten gold figures described in Ex. 25.18–22. Their wings were to spread out from each side over the cover of the Ark, traditionally known as the 'mercy seat' (RSV); *the place of expiation* (compare Heb. 2.17) of which God said: *It is there that I shall meet you* (Ex. 25.22). All this would be reassuring to the Jewish readers of Hebrews. The writer does not question that the old regulations for worship were ordained by God, or that the tabernacle and its contents were holy. On the contrary, he heaps up details to emphasize their value; but the new covenant is more glorious still. Paul reaches the same conclusion independently in II Corinthians 3.

Since vv. 1–5 contain the fullest description in the New Testament of the Old Testament sanctuary, the writer's statement that he is not to discuss them in detail may strike some readers as odd. By comparison with the Old Testament descriptions, however, Hebrews' references are indeed brief and selective.

9.6–10 moves from the setting of the sanctuary to its liturgy. At this point those readers of Hebrews whose churches either have no fixed forms of worship, or claim the right to change such forms from time to time, will have to adjust their thinking in two ways. On the one hand, they will need to enter sympathetically into the belief, doubtless shared by the writer and his readers, that every detail of the liturgy had been laid down by God himself, and communicated to Israel through angels (2.2) to Moses, so that nothing could be changed except by God himself (7.12). On the other hand, however, it may be reassuring for modern readers to realize that the Old Testament rules governing public worship, unlike most liturgies today, are more concerned with actions than with words. In this respect, they are in the same tradition as Jesus' '*Do* this, in memory of me'. Within the Old Testament, Deut. 26.3–10, where the words of a confession of faith are laid down, is a rare exception.

The whole of vv. 6–10 is a single sentence in Greek. Verses 6f. state the contrast between what happened in the outer and inner parts of the sanctuary; vv. 8f. explore the significance of this liturgy in the light of Christ; and v. 10 sums up this stage of the argument. This stage is essentially negative, showing the inadequacy of the old forms of worship; the positive phase of the argument will come in vv. 11–14.

The contrast between the liturgy of the outer and inner sanctuaries may be stated as follows:

outer	*inner*
priests	*high priest alone*
continually	*once a year*

Under this arrangement is literally 'these things having thus been set up', the verb used in v. 2. *Continually* is a pardonable exaggeration; Num. 18.2–6 refers in fact to sacrifices twice daily.

The simple scheme presented in the diagram is immediately complicated by three other factors. (1) Even the high priest has to offer sacrifice for his own sins as well as those of the people (see 7.27, and compare Lev. 9.7,16; 16.6,15). (2) Even the high priest's sacrifices on the great annual Day of Atonement can only deal with 'inadvertent' sins, of the kind described in Num. 15; for example, defilement by accidentally touching a corpse. (3) Less immediately important for the immediate argument, though the writer later (v. 22) emphasizes it as significant, the sacrifices are animal sacrifices, involving the shedding and sprinkling of blood. The result is an implied 'how much more' argument: these limitations on the scope of the Day of Atonement liturgy must apply still more to the less important daily sacrifices. The implied conclusion is plain: the old covenant cannot deal with sin.

9.8–10 The words *by this the Holy Spirit indicates . . .* and *all this is symbolic* mark a shift from the literal description of what went on in the sanctuary to the deeper meaning of that liturgy. The literal facts and the symbolic meaning are so different that the question immediately arises: 'What, then, does the old liturgy mean or do?' This question is answered in v. 10.

The Holy Spirit in Hebrews is seen, on the one hand, as speaking in Scripture (6.4; 10.15), and, on the other hand, as working in the lives of Christians (2.4; 6.4). These two aspects of the Spirit's work come together as the writer draws a negative conclusion from something which did not happen in worship under the old order: the people never reached 'the place where sins were forgiven' (9.5, GNB). True, the high priest went there on the Day of Atonement; but for the moment the writer keeps the significance of this positive fact in reserve, concentrating on the severe limitations of access to God under the old covenant.

The outer tent is literally 'the first tent' or tabernacle. Does this mean (1) first in place, the outer part of the tabernacle as opposed to the inner; or (2) first in time, the old or earthly tabernacle as a whole, as opposed to the new or heavenly one? Translations are divided: RSV and GNB, like REB, choose (1); NJB's 'the old tent' chooses (2); and NIV's literal 'the first tent' leaves both options open. The problem arises because the author is making a gradual transition from one phase in the argument to another; as he says himself, from literal description to symbolic meaning. If 'the first tent' is therefore to be understood in symbolic terms, NJB's 'the old tent' is to be preferred; the phrase will refer to the old tabernacle as a whole, contrasted with the new. This is confirmed by various other details. (a) Nowhere does the writer envisage a situation in which the material Holy Place or outer sanctuary would be destroyed, and the material Holy of Holies or inner sanctuary left standing. (b) Nowhere does he speak of a division between a Holy Place and a Holy of Holies in heaven (but see comment on v. 11). (c) The language of v. 8 is mainly temporal, not spatial: literally, *the way into the sanctuary has not yet been opened up; the first sanctuary still stands.*

If this is correct, *the way into the sanctuary* will mean 'the way into the real, heavenly sanctuary'. If the writer had meant 'the way into the Holy of Holies', he could have said so; but the description of the two-part earthly sanctuary in vv. 2f.,6f. has served its purpose and will not be used again. Its place is now taken by the greater contrast between the whole earthly sanctuary on the one hand, and 'heaven itself' (v. 24) on the other.

9.9 *All this* is literally 'which', and must grammatically refer to 'the first tent' (v. 8), which, it was argued above, means the old sanctuary as a whole.

Symbolic (also RSV; GNB, NJB 'a symbol'; NIV more weakly 'an illustration') is literally 'a parable', but the Greek word, and still more its Hebrew counterpart, are used for a range of analogies and proverbs much wider than the familiar gospel parables. In the New Testament, the word is only used outside the synoptic gospels here and in 11.19, in an adverbial phrase which RSV, NIV, and NJB translate 'figuratively speaking'.

In the phrase *it means, it* probably refers to the 'parable'; less probably to 'the first tent'; it makes little difference to the meaning of the sentence as a whole. In any case, under the old order *gifts and sacrifices* (the set phrase used in 5.1; 8.3) are offered.

The present time may mean the period in which the new covenant takes effect; but the context makes this most unlikely. *The present time* is the time during which the old, *external ordinances* are 'still in force until the coming of the new order' (v. 10).

The inadequacy of the old order is now brought home by the use of two of Hebrews' key words. The second, 'to perfect' or *bring to perfection* has been used before, and will be used again, of Christ's completing his own mission through his death (2.10; 5.9; 7.28; 10.14); it will be used of others whom he brings to perfection (11.40; 12.24); and it is used here, as in 10.1, of the powerlessness of the old order. The writer's repeated use of this word is directly linked with his concern that the readers should hold their faith fast *to the end* (3.14; 6.11); the Greek words for 'perfect' and 'end' are related.

The second key word is *conscience*, which is here used for the first time in Hebrews. As elsewhere in the New Testament, the word 'conscience' on its own normally means a bad conscience; if you want to refer to a 'good conscience', you have to say so, as the writer does in 13.18. Elsewhere he speaks of the cleansing of the conscience through the sacrifice of Christ (9.14; 10.22), or of the old order as unable to do this (here and in 10.2). In many languages the words for 'conscience' and 'consciousness' are the same or related; in the New Testament the conscience usually functions as a consciousness of sin.

Modern readers may feel, as they encounter this word *conscience*, that they are finally coming out of the fog of obscure theology into the clear daylight of moral values which they can understand. This is fine in itself; but Hebrews never presents the cleansed conscience as a purely subjective change of feeling. Just as the bad conscience is related to the objective fact of sin, so Hebrews links the subjective cleansed conscience with the objective, sacrificial death of Christ. The link between the two is faith (10.22). The principle remains valid, even under the new order, that forgiveness involves sacrifice (see comment on 9.22). Just as economists tell us that there are no free lunches, so Bonhoeffer taught that there is no 'cheap grace'. Indeed, there is no absolutely free grace: the grace which is free to us (4.16) has cost the sacrifice of Christ. Yet the language of cost, like all metaphors, is limited in scope; the Christ's sacrifice cannot be understood in less than personal terms, and this the writer to Hebrews will attempt later, especially in 10.5–10.

9.10   So what was the point of the old order? The question is important for the readers, for whom it was still a live option. It is *concerned only* (emphatic in the Greek) *with food and drink:* the kind of regulations listed in Lev. 11, one of the less dog-eared parts of most Christians' Bibles. The writer and his readers, like Jews (and some Jewish Christians) today, doubtless took these regulations seriously, but the point is that they do not affect the conscience, and therefore cannot complete the process of purification, or give the worshipper real access to God. The same is true of Old Testament *rites of cleansing,* of the kind mentioned, for example, in Lev. 11.25; 15.18; Num. 19.13 (the word translated *cleansing rites* in Heb. 6.2). 'Various' refers to the different situations in which such ritual cleansing was required: NJB translates 'washing at various times'; compare Mark 7.3f.and parallel.

Other religious traditions had, and still have, dietary rules and purification ceremonies. Although the writer of Hebrews is thinking primarily of the Old Testament laws, any non-Jewish Christians among the first readers could have found this verse speaking to their situation also. Modern Western readers should remind themselves of the point which the writer is making. Dietary rules and purification ceremonies are ineffective, he says, not, as we might think, because they belong to alien and inferior traditions; that was not the case for the writer and his first readers. They are ineffective because they do not preserve or maintain inward freedom from sin, or openness to God.

External ordinances in force until the coming of the new order are literally 'ordinances' (compare v. 1) 'of the flesh' (see comment on v. 13) 'established until a time of putting straight'. The word is not used elsewhere in the Greek Bible, but a related word is used in 12.12 of strengthening weak knees.

9.11–14   are mainly a positive statement of what Christ has done, though there are still elements of contrast with the old order, the value of which, perhaps perplexingly for some modern readers, is not entirely denied. The passage consists of two sentences in Greek: vv. 11f. contrast the ministry of Christ (vv. 11a,12b) with the old liturgy (vv. 11b,12a); vv. 13f. form a 'how much more' argument designed to show the superiority of Christ's sacrifice.

9.11   The name *Christ* is used alone and emphatically at the beginning of the sentence. Some have found it significant that it comes at the precise centre of Hebrews. However that may be, the writer has now reached the very heart of his theme. His argument is ultimately based, not on logical deductions, even from Scripture, but on facts; on what God has done. *Christ has come* to act as our high priest (compare 8.1); more precisely, *high priest of good things already in being*. NJB follows other manuscripts in its translation 'all the blessings which were to come'; compare footnotes in REB and other translations. It is likely that the scribes who copied these manuscripts were unduly influenced by the phrase *the good things to come* in 10.1. The fact that the writer probably used both expressions illustrates the 'overlap of the ages' mentioned in the introduction to this section. What these *good things* are can be discovered by looking back to v. 9 (*a clear conscience* and being brought to perfection), or forward to the second part of v. 14, where however the blessings are still spoken of as future.

It is helpful to compare REB's translation of vv. 11b and 12a with a more literal translation such as RSV or NIV. The main line of the sentence may be translated literally as follows, largely on the basis of RSV: 'Christ entered once for all into the Holy Place *through* the greater and more perfect tent, not *through* the blood of goats and calves but *through* his own blood.' The word translated 'through', in Greek as in English, may mean, either 'by way of' or 'by means of'. Not everyone agrees, but it seems most natural to understand the first 'through' as meaning 'by way of', and the second and third 'through's as meaning 'by means of'. If so, the picture is one of Christ rising through a heavenly tabernacle into the immediate presence of God. There is however no speculation about various divisions or circles in heaven (see comment on 4.14). As the hymn puts it, rather more specifically than Hebrews, Christ rose

> Through all ranks of creatures
> To the central height,
> To the throne of Godhead,
> To the Father's breast.[1]

The heavenly tabernacle, essentially *heaven itself* (v. 24, an essential commentary on the present verse), was made by God, not by (human) hands. This contrast, already mentioned in 8.2, will recur in 9.24, and underlies the references to a heavenly country or city in 11.14ff.

---

[1] Caroline Maria Noel, 'At the name of Jesus'; *HP* 74.

The whole argument about Christ's high priesthood reaches its culmination at this point. He is 'a different kind of priest' (7.11); although the levitical priests were also *called by God* (5.4), the difference in Jesus' priesthood is that it belongs to heaven and is now exercised in heaven. Notwithstanding the reality of his earthly life (2.9) and death (12.2), his ministry does not of its nature belong *to this created world*. Jesus says the same thing in different words, for example in John 17.6,16; 18.36.

9.12   If the place of Christ's sacrifice is different, so also is what is offered. It is not any more the blood of animals (the animals are different in v. 13, but the writer does not worry about such details), but his own blood. Sometimes, both in Catholic and Protestant traditions, the blood of Christ has been treated as an object separate from Christ himself. On the contrary, it is essential to the thought of Hebrews that the blood should be understood as standing for the voluntary sacrificial death (see 10.5–10) of Christ *himself* (v. 14).

That sacrifice is offered *once for all*; a theme already announced in 7.27, and most fully discussed in 9.26–28. Hebrews links repetition with ineffectiveness; conversely, what is effectively done once need never be done again. The *liberation* which his sacrifice effects is *eternal*. That is, on the one hand, it has its source in the eternal world (cf. *eternal Spirit* in v. 14); and, on the other hand, it is permanent.

The 'how much more' argument of *vv. 13f.* is likely to cause problems for some modern readers, since they do not share the first readers' assumption that sprinkling animals' blood and ashes can make people pure. The argument is however consistent on its own terms. The writer is not even saying to his first readers: 'If, as you claim, . . . blood . . . consecrates . . .'. He himself has just conceded to the old sacrifices the status of *external ordinances* (literally, 'ordinances of the flesh') *in force until the coming of the new order* (v. 10). The end of v. 13, literally, 'for the purification of the flesh', repeats the key word 'flesh'.

In his references to various animals, the writer clearly has Old Testament sacrifices in mind, but he does not quote any particular text. In Num. 19.1, 'the ashes of the cow' are ordered to be collected and deposited outside the Israelite camp; in v. 4, the cow's blood, not its ashes, is to be sprinkled 'towards the front of the Tent of Meeting'; see also vv. 17ff. But the writer is probably thinking mainly of the great Day of Atonement described in Lev. 16; see particularly vv. 3,14f.

9.14   Christ's sacrifice is in total contrast with all this, except for two features which form the common ground on which the contrast is built. First, the writer uses of Christ a word meaning *without blemish*, not used elsewhere in Hebrews (compare similar language in 7.26), but which in the Old Testament (e.g. Num. 28–29) is frequently applied to animal sacrifices. Second, the sacrifice of Christ, like sacrifices under the old order, was *offered . . . to God*.

The points of contrast are as follows:

(1) Animal sacrifices purify the flesh; Christ's sacrifice was made *through the eternal Spirit*. This is almost certainly a reference to the Holy Spirit, not to Christ's own spirit. *Eternal* in Hebrews overlaps considerably in meaning with 'heavenly', and indicates that which has its 'place' with God in the world which cannot be shaken (12.25–29).

(2) Christ offered, not an animal, but himself; he is both high priest and sacrifice. His sacrifice is therefore an act of his own will (compare 10.5–10).

(3) As already stated in vv. 10 and 13, the old sacrifices have to do only with physical, ritual, external purity; Christ's sacrifice purifies the conscience, that is, the inner person (see comment on 6.1).

(4) The old ritual did not give worshippers access to the living God; this is now possible through the sacrifice of Christ. *The deadness of our former ways* is literally 'dead works'. Sometimes this set phrase means 'acts which lead to death'. This may be the meaning here, in which case it will be the same as the 'sins committed under the former covenant' mentioned in v. 15. Alternatively, the meaning may be '(ritual) acts which do not lead to life' (see comment on 6.1); GNB translates 'useless rituals'. Similarly, the phrase 'the living God' is sometimes used in speaking of judgment (3.12; 10.31); but more often God is spoken of as the source of life (10.20; 12.22; compare 12.9; 4.12 combines both negative and positive aspects in speaking of God's word).

(5) The contrast of tense between *consecrates* in v. 13, speaking of the old order, and *will cleanse* here, in speaking of the new, is not emphasized. The first readers were probably intended to understand that although the new order was already here in Christ, it was still an open question whether or not they would themselves obtain its benefits. See the introduction to this section.

For *our conscience,* some manuscripts have 'your conscience', as in RSV text. The words for 'our' and 'your' are pronounced the same in Greek, and are often confused.

Serve is the word translated *minister* in 8.5, and 'worship' in 12.28; NJB translates it as 'worship' here. Here the context shows that the writer is thinking primarily of worship, and that is how he always uses the word. When he speaks of Christian service, as in 10.24; 13.1ff., he uses different language.

Verses 15–22 deepen what has been said, first about the new order (v. 15) and then about the old (vv. 18–21). There is no major new development, but vv. 16f. add an illustration of the meaning of *covenant*, and v. 22 states a principle underlying sacrifice in general. Verses 15ff. are concerned with death, and vv. 18–22 more specifically with blood; but the two are closely connected in the wider context.

In 9.15 the writer gathers together various aspects of the previous argument. (1) Christ (implied) is the mediator (8.6) of a new covenant. (2) A death has taken place – clearly Christ's (9.14). (3) The result of this death is, negatively, *to bring liberation* (a word related to that used in v. 12) *from sins* (more precisely, infringements of the law) *committed under the former* (literally 'first') *covenant* (perhaps the 'dead works' mentioned in v. 14). (4) To put it positively, Christ's death makes it possible for *those whom God has called to receive* (literally, 'inherit'; see 1.2) *the eternal* (compare vv. 12,14) *inheritance* which God *has promised them:* that is, the 'place of rest' with God discussed in 3.7–4.11, and the new covenant foretold by Jeremiah (see 8.7–13). These are the enefits of Christ's death which the writer does not want his readers to miss through any neglect or failure in endurance.

9.16f. illustrate the meaning of *covenant* by a play on two senses of the Greek word, which also means 'will' or *testament*. The argument is not entirely arbitrary: both God's covenant and a human will are unilateral acts by which something is promised or given to someone else. Yet the two senses are distinct, and it is right to translate them differently; GNB, for example, has a note on 'covenant' in v. 18 reading: 'In Greek the same word means "will" and "covenant".' The parallel between the two senses of the word is in any case limited: the death of a testator is not sacrificial, and does not have to be violent.

Early editions of GNB translated v. 16 with beautiful simplicity: 'In the case of a will it is necessary to prove that the man who made it has died.' More recent editions have 'person' instead of 'man'. It is in fact unlikely that women could make wills in Judaism at this time, though in certain circumstances they could inherit property (see

Num. 27.6ff.). This, however, is not the point at issue, which concerns the death of the testator.

9.18   Unusually for Hebrews, the transition from the illustration of the will back to the main argument about the covenant is rather awkward: more so than REB suggests. This verse, like v. 22, is concerned with general principles underlying sacrifice. Literally translated, the verse reads: 'Hence neither was the first [covenant] inaugurated without blood.' The following argument requires the meaning *covenant*; and *blood*, as usual in Hebrews, means not 'death' in general, but 'sacrificial death'. The illustration of the will is soon left behind; it is indeed of limited value.

9.19   The writer turns back to the familiar ground of Scripture; common ground between himself and his readers. The first covenant, like the second, was inaugurated by sacrifice: in the case of the first, by many animal sacrifices. The reference is mainly to Ex. 24.3,6ff., supplemented by Lev. 14.4. Compare also Num. 19.6, which mentions 'marjoram' or hyssop 'and scarlet thread'; but these passages refer to a different event, not the establishment of the Sinai covenant with which Ex. 24 is concerned.

The writer of Hebrews emphasizes that *all the commandments* were read *to all the people*, and that Moses sprinkled *all the people* and *all the vessels* (v. 21). As in 9.1–5, he does not stress the value of the new order by devaluing the old covenant, on which, for most of his readers, their status as God's special people rested. Paul follows a similar approach in Rom. 3.1f. and 9.4f.

Many manuscripts add 'and goats' after *calves*; they are followed by RSV, GNB, and NJB.

9.20   Moses' words are quoted with some differences from the Hebrew and the Greek. The quotation begins: *This is*, different from the beginning of Ex. 24.8, which is literally 'behold'; this may reflect Jesus' words of institution at the Last Supper (Mark 14.24 and parallels). The Greek text has 'the Lord' instead of 'God', and uses a word for 'made' which is related to the word for 'covenant', and which Hebrews never uses of the old covenant. Instead, Hebrews has *commanded* (*to keep* is implied).

9.21   adds more details from Lev. 8.15,19, which is not part of the story of the inauguration of the Sinai covenant. The writer tends to work with a generalized picture of Old Testament worship rather than draw significance from minor details.

9.22   shows the same tendency: the word *almost* covers a wide range of objects which are not cleansed by blood. More important, and more difficult, is the last part of the verse. The problem is to know whether (a) it applies only to what happens *under the law*, or whether (b) the writer understands it as a universal principle. GNB and NJB appear to choose the first alternative; other translations, including REB, leave the matter open. The words *under the law* are rather emphatic, but this does not settle the question of whether they cover the whole verse, or just its first part. The word for *forgiveness* is used in 10.18 of forgiveness under the new covenant, but the statement in 9.22b appears quite general; the author seems to expect his readers to accept it without discussion. The strongest argument in favour of (b) is that the principle does in fact apply, in the writer's thinking, both to Old Testament sacrifices and to the sacrifice of Christ (see especially 10.10). But the principle is valid only in the setting of human beings approaching God in worship; the author is not claiming that blood must be involved when one human being forgives another. The statement is nevertheless strange to most modern ears. As elsewhere (2.10; 7.26), the author moves from what God has done in Christ to explaining how such action was appropriate. Here he is, as it were, calling on the Old Testament sacrifices to confirm the fitness of Christ's sacrificial death.

9.23 – 10.18   *Jesus, the final sacrifice*

If the previous section was the heart of Hebrews' argument, this section is its conclusion. The rest of the letter will not contain any sustained doctrinal teaching, but will concentrate mainly on the writer's appeal to his readers to hold firm in their faith.

Even this section is far from offering entirely fresh teaching; on the contrary, it builds on the entire previous argument, without declining into mere repetition. In particular, 10.5–10, while still moving within the category of sacrifice, transcends it by stressing the voluntary, willing nature of Christ's sacrifice. This, in the last analysis, is what sets it apart from and above all animal sacrifice, and declares the new order to supersede the old.

In 9.23–28   the writer first returns to the picture drawn in 8.5, of a universe in which earthly symbols reflect heavenly realities.

He begins with a difficult statement which he then explains. *9.23* presents another 'how much more' argument. The old liturgy, as he has just said, involved sprinkling blood over *almost . . . everything* used in worship (vv. 19–22), in order to make things ritually pure. But the old liturgy is only the earthly copy of the worship of heaven. It follows logically that the heavenly realities require to be cleansed by greater or better sacrifices than those offered under the old order.

If we were reading this passage on its own, it would be natural to think it meant that Christ must continually repeat his sacrifice in heaven, so that the one sacrifice on earth becomes, so to speak, a multiplicity of *better sacrifices* in heaven. As if to correct this possible misunderstanding, the writer will state with overwhelming emphasis in vv. 26–28 that Christ's sacrifice was offered *once for all*. As the 1662 *Book of Common Prayer* put it, with comparable emphasis, he made on the cross '(by his one oblation of himself once offered) a full, perfect, and sufficient sacrifice, oblation, and satisfaction for the sins of the whole world'. The *better sacrifices* of v. 23 must therefore be understood generally, as a better counterpart (soon to be specified) to the old sacrifices; NJB translates 'a higher sort of sacrifice', and this gives the meaning.

But why should the *heavenly things themselves* require cleansing? NJB's note probably gives the right explanation: 'The "purification" of the sanctuary, whether the earthly or the heavenly one, does not necessarily imply any previous "impurity". It is a consecratory and inaugural rite.' The writer is thinking for the moment, not of Christ's death in itself, as a historical event, but of the effects of that death. These effects are nothing less than cosmic, reconsecrating heaven itself, and opening it up to sinners who, for their part, have been more than ritually purified.

9.24   begins by going back over old ground, as all good preachers need to do at times (compare 8.2; 9.11). He then states more clearly in what Jesus' continuing ministry in heaven consists: he is in God's presence, interceding on our behalf (compare 7.22; Rom. 8.34; I John 2.1).

In 9.25   the words translated: *It was not his purpose to offer himself . . .* may also mean: *The result was not that he offered himself . . .* , or more generally, as in most translations: 'It was not that he offered himself again and again', as in the annual Day of Atonement ritual.

9.26   If Jesus' sacrifice were to be repeatable, the result would be absurd: he would have had to suffer (and *suffer*, as usual in Hebrews, implies 'die') many times since the creation. We might have expected the writer to say: 'He would have to die again and again until the end of time'; but as 1.2 showed, the significance of Christ stretches back to creation, as well as forward to the end.

Now comes a concentrated positive statement. In fact, Christ has *appeared* once for all on earth to deal with human sin 'by sacrificing himself' (NJB). The form of the verb translated *appeared* suggests that, although the sacrifice itself took place at a particular time, its results are lasting. The phrase which REB boldly translates *at the climax of history* recalls 'this the final age' in 1.2; literally, 'at the completion of the ages'. Matthew speaks similarly of the 'completion of the age' (*the end of time*, 13.39f.,49; 28.20; *the end of the age*, 24.3); and Daniel of *the time of the end* (12.4) or *the end of the age* (12.13). The writer of Hebrews, like other New Testament writers, is convinced that, although time has not yet come to a stop, the coming of Christ is so momentous that God has nothing comparable left to do. It was natural to conclude from this that *we see the day of the Lord drawing near* (Heb. 10.25), but such texts as Mark 13.32f. show Christians aware of the danger of exact predictions about the time of the end.

9.27f.   begin with a comparison which cannot be pressed too far between Christ's death *'once* for all', and the fact that everyone must die once. The human side of the comparison may be either an appeal to general experience or an echo of Gen. 3.19 or both. On the human side, death is followed by judgment: again, a belief which needs no discussion, because the readers would accept it implicitly. On the side of Christ, death is an offering *to bear the sins of mankind*, literally 'the sins of many'. This is probably an echo of Isa. 53.12. 'Many' does not imply 'not everyone', but that a great number of people were involved, not just one or a few (compare Mark 10.45 and parallel).

So what, for Christ, is still to come (as judgment is still to come for others)? Not a dealing with sin, for that has been done once for all, but the final salvation (compare Rom. 13.11, REB 'deliverance') of those who, when he returns, will be found still eagerly awaiting him (compare Matt. 25.1–13). This verse is the nearest the New Testament comes to speaking of Christ's 'second coming'.

By now the first readers would be able to relate their own situation to this description of the end, and to the warning of 6.4–6. There is no more that can or need be done, on God's side, to deal with sin. There is no other effective sacrifice but Christ's, and that is past. The present is the time of Christ's ministry of intercession, and of believers' patient expectancy. The future is the time of Christ's return in glory, and of believers' final salvation if they keep faith to the end.

10.1–18   is divided by REB and others into three paragraphs. (GNB and NIV begin a fourth paragraph with v. 15.) The first paragraph (vv. 1–4) appears on first reading largely negative and repetitious, but it leads to a statement essential to the argument. If, on the one hand, *without the shedding of blood there is no forgiveness* (9.22), and on the other hand, 'it is impossible for the blood of bulls and goats to take away sins' (10.4, NIV), then it follows that only a human sacrifice (that is, Christ's, for no other human sacrifice is even considered) can take away sins.

The second paragraph (vv. 5–10), built around a quotation of Ps. 40.6ff., calls Scripture itself to witness that what God requires is not animal sacrifice but obedient submission to his will – something that Christ perfectly accomplished in the offering of his body on the cross. The category of sacrifice is not left behind, so there is (as always in Hebrews) continuity between the old and the new. It is however transcended and transformed in the sacrifice of Christ, which cleanses 'us' (v. 10) from sin, and thus sets us apart for the willing service of God.

The third paragraph (vv. 11–18) contrasts once again the many old sacrifices with the one effective sacrifice of Christ. It points once more to his exaltation; emphasizes the effect of his sacrifice in dealing with sin; and clinches the argument with a repeated quotation of Jer. 31.33f. (compare Heb. 8.10,12). A comment underlines the final words of the quotation: sins have now been forgiven, so sin-offerings are past.

10.1   Verses 1–2 form a single sentence in Greek. It is probably a rhetorical question. GNB translates the end of v. 1: 'How can the Law, then, by means of these sacrifices make perfect the people who come to God?' The implied answer is clearly that there is no way in which the law can do that; so other translations have a negative statement here.

The law, as always in Hebrews, means the Mosaic rules governing worship, particularly animal sacrifice. 'But' (GNB, NIV 'only') is implied. 'Shadow' is the word translated 'shadowy' in 8.5.

The good things to come are no doubt in content the same as the *good things already in being* mentioned in 9.11. These are essentially forgiveness of sins (10.17f.), access to God (10.19), perfection (10.14), and consecration to God (10.10,14). These are different aspects of the same new reality of life in Christ. But how can the same blessings be both *to come* and *already in being?* There are three possible answers.

The first is to explain 9.11 in the light of 10.1, as many scribes did by simply changing 9.11 so that the text read *good things to come* in both places. A less drastic means of reaching the same result is to argue that the 'good things' are, so to speak, virtually in being, or *reserved in heaven* (I Peter 1.4). This involves some watering down of 9.11.

The second solution is the converse of the first: to explain 10.1 in the light of 9.11, as NJB does by translating 'the good things which were still to come'. This is by no means impossible, and fits in well with the context, which speaks of the old order.

The third solution, adopted by most translations, assumes that the writer was using two different expressions in 9.11 and 10.1 to refer to present and future aspects of the same reality. Because Christians live in the 'overlap of the ages', they already enjoy the 'innumerable benefits which by his precious blood-shedding he hath obtained for us' (1662 *Book of Common Prayer*). Yet they do not have these benefits in all their fullness, and they can still lose them (10.26–31). Not only the Old Testament believers (11.16), but also Christians, are still *seekers after the city which is to come* (13.14).

The Greek word translated *true picture* is *eikon* (English 'icon' or 'ikon'), now used in the Eastern churches of stylized pictures of Christ or one of the saints, believed to participate in the holiness of what they represent. In the New Testament the word is used in various ways: of the image of a Roman emperor on a coin (Mark 12.16 and parallels); of the 'image of the beast', idolatrously worshipped in Revelation (13.14f. and often); of Christ as the perfect image or likeness of God (I Cor. 11.7; II Cor. 4.4; Col. 1.15); and of Christians as they grow like Christ (Rom. 8.29; compare I John 3.2), and through him like God (Col. 3.10; compare I Cor. 15.49). Hebrews uses the word only here; and only here, in the New Testament, is it used of something other than a person. The context suggests that it means *the real sanctuary* (8.2), as opposed to Moses' copy of it. NIV is therefore probably right in excluding any suggestion of its being 'only an image'; it translates 'the realities themselves'.

As previously noted, the writer of Hebrews' main concern is with the Old Testament order as a whole, not with distinctions between one ceremony and another. Here and in v. 3, when he writes *year after year*, he is doubtless thinking of the annual Day of Atonement ritual, referred to in 9.6f., and performed by the high priest alone.

But in v. 11, he moves on without any suggestion of contrast to speak of the 'daily' offerings which any priest could make. The point in both places is the same: the ritual is endlessly repeated, whether in a yearly or a daily cycle, without accomplishing what it at best prefigures.

The phrase *for all time* is used here of the old sacrifices, in 7.3 of Melchizedek, and in 10.12 of Christ's sacrifice; the same phrase is translated *for ever* in 10.14, referring to believers. A different phrase, also translated *for ever*, is used whenever Hebrews quotes or refers to Ps. 110.4 (for example, in 5.6; 7.28); also of Christ in 13.7. The two expressions are probably used for variety, with no difference of meaning.

10.2   The old law and its sacrifices do not achieve their end of wiping away sin and so opening up the way to God. The fact that they are indefinitely repeated shows their ineffectiveness. The underlying assumption is that one effective sacrifice would have been enough for all time. The writer is clearly arguing back from the one effective sacrifice of Christ, which he believes was in fact enough for all time. It is unlikely that the Old Testament sacrifices were ever thought of as having an effect which lasted beyond the time at which they were offered: their purpose was to wipe away past sins.

An expanded translation of this verse might run: 'But in fact the same sacrifices continue to be offered. This shows that the worshippers have not been cleansed once for all; they still feel a sense of sin.' GNB translates: 'If the people worshipping God had really been purified from their sins, they would not feel guilty of sin any more, and all sacrifices would stop.' The word translated 'feel' (*sense*) is translated 'conscience' in 9.9 and elsewhere; here it means 'consciousness' of sins.

10.3   Paradoxically, all that the old sacrifices do is to remind worshippers, year after year, that their sins are still with them. Once again (and there will be another example in vv. 5–10) the Old Testament order itself points to its own inadequacy, and so indirectly points forward to Christ. This is not the same as Paul's argument, for example in Rom. 7.7–12, that the moral law, by defining sins, actually stimulates the desire to commit them, and so leads the sinner to turn to God. This line of thought was developed by Calvin, who called it 'the first office of the law', quoting Augustine's prayer:

'Command what cannot be fulfilled, unless by thy own grace.'[1] But Paul's thought and Hebrews' converge on the basic fact of the law's inability to deal with sin. In this respect, the writer of Hebrews would have agreed with Paul that Christ is *the end of the law . . . for everyone who has faith* (Rom. 10.4).

Brought to mind translates a noun used elsewhere in the New Testament only in Jesus' words at the Last Supper: 'Do this as a memorial of me' (Luke 22.19, REB margin; compare I Cor. 11.24f.). It is tempting but speculative to see an echo of these words here.

10.4   This important verse states simply something which may seem obvious to a modern Western reader who has never practised animal sacrifice. The writer of Hebrews, on the contrary, has had to lead up to this statement with infinite care, otherwise he would have risked alienating his Jewish Christian readers. As recently as 9.13f. the argument still ran: 'If animal sacrifices cleanse worshippers from bodily defilement, how much more effective is the sacrifice of Christ!' Now, at last, the 'how much more' argument is laid aside, and the writer states boldly that in dealing with sin animal sacrifices have no power at all. The entire system of worship which God once set up, on which the readers once exclusively relied, and to which some of them are tempted to return, has been made ineffective by the very human sin which it was set up to deal with. It cannot make worshippers clean from individual sins, because God's whole people has committed the ultimate sin of unfaithfulness to God. God has therefore now set up a new covenant based on the sacrifice of Christ. To this, in the next paragraph (vv. 5–10), the writer now turns.

10.5–7   Anyone who has read ch. 1 attentively will be used by now to the writer's way of re-applying to Christ Old Testament texts which in their original setting referred to someone else. Psalm 40, called a psalm *for David* or 'of David' (NRSV), consists of a prayer of thanksgiving (vv. 1–10) and a lament (vv. 11–17) by an individual who is not named, except possibly in the heading, which is later than the psalm itself. The writer of Hebrews wastes no time on the possible attribution to David. For him the voice which speaks in these lines is Christ's. He is so convinced of this, and expects so confidently that his readers will agree, that he does not even name Christ in introducing the quotation: 'That is why he said, on coming into the world . . .' (NJB).

[1] *Institutes of the Christian Religion*, II.vii.6–9.

The world is clearly this world, not the heavenly world referred to in 2.5 and probably in 1.6, for which a different word is used. From beginning to end the incarnation is the story of a willing sacrifice.

He says here and in v. 8, and *he adds* (literally, 'has said') in v. 9, may grammatically mean 'it' (that is, Scripture) 'says' or 'has said'; but it is more natural to take these words as referring to Christ speaking in the psalm. GNB's 'he said to God' makes the meaning clear.

Ps. 40.6–8 are quoted with some differences from the Greek and the Hebrew. (1) Ps. 40.6 in Hebrew ends: 'Ears you have dug for me', which REB correctly takes to mean: *You have given me receptive ears.* The writer of Hebrews follows his Greek Old Testament text, which read 'but you have prepared a body for me.' The Greek for 'ears' could have been misread as 'body'. (2) *Whole-offerings and sin-offerings* in v. 6 is singular in the Hebrew of Ps. 40.6 ('burnt offering and sin offering'. RSV), but Hebrews probably follows Greek manuscripts which have the plural. The meaning in any case is the same, since the text refers to sacrifice in general, not to any one particular sacrifice. (3) *Delight in*, literally 'desire' (RSV), is weaker than the corresponding *demanded* in Ps. 40.6. (4) Hebrews condenses Ps. 40.7f., suggesting more strongly that Christ 'came' to earth to do God's will.

The verses quoted are one of a number of passages in the Old Testament which are sometimes understood to mean that sacrifices in themselves are useless. Similar texts include I Sam. 15.22 (where sacrifice is contrasted with obedience, as here); Pss. 50.8–14; 51.16f.; 69.30f.; Isa. 1. 11ff.; Jer. 7.21f.; Hos. 6.6; Amos 5.21f.; Micah 6.6ff. It is more likely that such texts mean that sacrifice is useless, not in itself, but if it is not accompanied by obedience to God. The Isaiah passage, for example, goes on to state that God will not listen to his people's prayers either as long as Israel remains in revolt against him; yet nowhere is it suggested that the prophet condemns prayer as such. If this is so, the difference between the Old Testament writers and what the writer of Hebrews has said so far may be explained as one of degree; but stronger language is coming in v. 9. The new factor in Hebrews is the perfect obedience of Christ, which makes forgiveness possible for those who trust him.

Hebrews does not comment on *the scroll*, literally 'the roll of the book' (RSV), so we do not know what the writer thought it was. Nor is this clear in the psalm. Some have taken it to be Deuteronomy, others the law of Moses as a whole, others a book kept in heaven.

10.8   comments on the lines quoted in vv. 5f.; 10.9 will comment on the quotation in v. 7. The first part of the quotation is condensed, and *sacrifices and offerings* are now mentioned in the plural, with no difference of meaning. The comment at the end of v. 8 is literally 'which are offered according to the law', but REB probably brings out the meaning. Even though God set up the old system of worship, in present circumstances he does not want its sacrifices.

In 10.9   *then he adds* builds on *then I said* in the quotation. The rest of the quotation, already selective in v. 7, is further condensed to make the point still sharper. The comment which follows points up the contrast between the two halves of the quotation. They refer in fact to the old order which God now *abolishes*, and the new order which he establishes. *Abolishes* is the strongest language the writer ever uses, perhaps the strongest he could use, about the end of the old order. The same word is used in Matt. 2.16 of the 'massacre' of baby boys in Bethlehem, and in II Thess. 2.8 of the Lord Jesus annihilating the wicked one. Even here, however, the writer is not making an abstract statement to the effect that animal sacrifice is useless: he is pointing to an act by which God put an end to a system which he had himself set up.

The word for *establish* means literally 'stand'; is used in v. 11 in its literal meaning. Here, however, two ideas are probably combined: first, the inauguration of the new order (compare v. 20); and second, its absolute security, even when everything else is being shaken (an idea developed in 12.26–29).

10.10 is tightly packed: literally, 'by which will we have been consecrated through the offering of the body of Jesus Christ once for all'. On the meaning of *consecrated*, see the comment on 2.11. 'Offering' is the word used in vv. 5,8 of animal sacrifices. But what is this *will?* From one point of view it is the will of God, which Christ came to do. But from another point of view it is also the will of Christ himself, without which the will of God could have done nothing for believers. The two wills become perfectly one in Christ's perfect obedience. On this basis, GNB's apparently free translation can be generally justified:

> Because Jesus Christ did what God wanted him to do, we are all purified from sin by the offering that he made of his own body once and for all.

The first 'all', however, is not in the text.

10.11–18 This, the final paragraph of Hebrews in which doctrinal teaching predominates, consists (1) of a summary contrast between the old priests (v. 11) and Christ (vv. 12f.), and (2) a quotation which, together with a brief comment, brings the argument to a close.

The contrast in vv. 11ff. may be outlined as follows:

1	*Every priest*	*Christ*
2	*stands*	*took his seat+*
3	*performing his service*	*having offered*
4	*time after time*	*for all time*
5	*the same sacrifices*	*a single sacrifice**
6	*which can never remove sins*	*for sins**

The second part of the contrast is more important and therefore longer (compare 1.1–4). The point marked + indicates further development in vv. 12f.; the points marked * indicate further development in v. 14.

Line 1 implies that Christ too is a priest, indeed a high priest; but the writer has said this so often since 2.17 that he does not need to repeat it here. (Some scribes actually wrote 'every high priest', no doubt from force of habit; but since the writer is now thinking of the daily sacrifices, this is almost certainly wrong.) There is therefore both explicit contrast and implied comparison here.

Line 2 implies contrast: for the priest to stand implies that he still has work to do. The difference in tense underlines the contrast: Christ's saving work is finished.

The same is true of the tenses in line 3; otherwise this line provides the main basis for the comparison. Line 4 is contrast. Lines 5 and 6 contain both comparison and contrast: in both the old and the new order, there are sacrifices to do with sin; but otherwise they are quite different.

So much is summary of the great doctrinal passage which has stretched from the beginning of chapter 7. But there is more.

(1) All this largely fresh and sometimes difficult (5.11) teaching is, as it were, sewn back into the canvas of the whole letter by reference to the theme of Christ's exaltation with which the letter began (1.3f.), and to that of his continuing ministry in heaven (7.25) which is a necessary complement to his once-for-all sacrifice. His 'waiting' is to be understood as active. The relation between the once-for-all sacrifice and the continuing ministry was defined in 9.28.

(2) The conclusion of the whole matter is that Christ has made believers fit to worship God: by his sacrifice they are *consecrated* (v. 10), *perfected* (v. 14), and *forgiven* (v. 18). To show what this means in

practice for the readers will be the main purpose of the rest of Hebrews.

10.12   *Christ* is literally and respectfully 'this one'; he has been named in v. 10, and there can be no doubt about who is meant.

Most translations, like REB, connect the words *for all time* with Christ's sacrifice; GNB's 'an offering that is effective forever' brings out the meaning. NJB, however, links the words 'for all time' with Christ's sitting at God's right hand: he has 'taken his seat for ever, at the right hand of God'. This is grammatically possible, but the words 'for ever' are not part of the allusion to Ps. 110.1. Moreover, NJB comes near to contradicting the following words, about Christ *now* waiting *until his enemies are made his footstool*. The word *until* does not of itself mean that once Christ's enemies are defeated, he will stand up again and enter a new period of activity; but this is strongly suggested in 7.28.

Are made, literally 'they make', is a reverent way of saying 'God makes', as comparison with Ps. 110.1 shows.

Greek past tenses normally indicate whether an event took place at a particular time in the past, or whether its effects continue into the present. The verbs in v. 12 have the first form; *has perfected* in v. 14 has the second.

10.15–18   The second quotation from Jer. 31, now reduced to parts of vv. 33f., is not mere repetition. The point, when this passage was first quoted in Heb. 8.8–12, was that a new covenant was needed, that God had promised one, and that now it had been established, it automatically made the first covenant old. Now, the point is that this new covenant has effected forgiveness of sins, thereby making any other sin-offering superfluous. Stress therefore falls on the last line of the quotation. This is shown mainly by the comment in v. 18, but also by the way in which the quotation is arranged. This is literally, (v. 15) 'after having said, "This is the covenant" . . .' '*and* "their sins and their wicked deeds I will remember no more." ' The and which we have underlined is actually part of the quotation. The writer uses it to mean then he adds, drawing attention to the final words. REB unnecessarily translates it twice.

As elsewhere (see comment on 3.7), the Holy Spirit is seen as speaking in Scripture. *Adds his witness* is literally 'also witnesses to us'. The previous argument is complete in itself, since it is based essentially on what God has done; but the words of Jeremiah confirm it.

10.19–39   *Let us come near to God*

No part of Hebrews shows more plainly than this passage that the writer's concern is not with abstract theological teaching but with his readers' eternal destiny. If he had been purely writing a treatise on the person and work of Christ, he could have stopped at 10.18; for on this theme, he has gathered up the threads of the argument, and he will have nothing further to say. Instead, the first two paragraphs of this section bring together, in contrast still painful to read, one of his most moving passages of encouragement (vv. 19–25), and a warning (vv. 26–31) which is in some ways even sterner than 6.4ff. The rest of the section (vv. 32–39) begins as a comparatively low-key appeal to the readers' own memory and experience, which broadens out into a promise from Scripture (Hab. 2.3f.)

The whole of *10.19–25* is a single sentence in Greek. Is it too fanciful to suggest that the writer's determined control of his syntax reflects his determination to hold on to his readers' minds and hearts? Perhaps not, if even handwriting can show a person's character. Modern English, however, prefers shorter sentences, so current translations divide the passage into two (RSV), three (NRSV), four (NIV), five (REB), six (NJB), or eight (GNB) sentences.

10.19f.   *So now* is literally 'therefore' (RSV): the appeal follows on from the theology. *My friends* is literally 'brothers' (NIV), but sisters are not excluded. The author uses this word, more sparingly than Paul and other New Testament writers, to awaken his readers' attention to a word of encouragement (as here and in 3.1; 13.22) or warning (as in 3.12); but also to recall that fellow-Christians are members of the same family (see 2.10–18). He does not here make the further point that Christians are brothers and sisters of Christ, or say that they are priests under Christ, their high priest. What he does say is that through death and exaltation to his Father's right hand, Jesus has opened up or inaugurated a new way to life, that is, into the presence of God, for others.

So much is clear; but some details are difficult. The main problems are as follows.

(1) The *sanctuary*, literally, 'holy [place]' is probably to be understood in general terms, as meaning the presence of God. 12.22–24

will eloquently express how close he believes Christian worship to come to sharing in the worship of heaven. The readers still live by faith (v.22), not by sight; they still need to be encouraged to walk freely (v. 19) and steadfastly (v. 23) along the path of God which Jesus has cleared. But nothing here marks the distinction made in 9.2f. between an inner and an outer sanctuary, or suggests that believers enter only the outer chamber. On the contrary, the writer's intention is that the readers shall follow Jesus to the end, both in time and on their spiritual journey.

(2) Verse 20 is literally 'which he has inaugurated for us, a way new and living through the curtain, that is of his flesh'. The problem is to know whether *his flesh* is identified (a) with the *way* or (b) with *the curtain*.

If (a) is correct, the picture will be that the sacrifice of Christ's flesh (or body, 10.10) opened up a way through the *curtain* which until then separated humanity from God. That is how REB understands it, and this is the simpler explanation. It is made clearer still if the end of the verse is understood, as it may be, to mean '. . . a way through the curtain, that is by means of his flesh'; but this is not absolutely necessary.

Most translations, however, appear to choose (b). Some may do this passively, by following more closely the order of the Greek words. GNB does so by conscious choice: 'He opened for us a new way, a living way, through the curtain – that is, through his own body.' In favour of this is that it is a somewhat more natural way of understanding the Greek. Against it are the awkward identification of Christ's body with a curtain, and the further question of whether the curtain is thought of as an obstacle, or, more naturally (once it has been torn, cf. Mark 15.38 and parallels), as a way of access.

Neither explanation is easy; but on the whole option (a), the REB understanding, may be preferred.

In v. 20, *new* translates an unusual word, not used elsewhere in Hebrews. Outside the Bible, it is sometimes used of freshly killed animal sacrifices. This sense, though tempting, is unlikely here; the corresponding adverb in Acts 18.2 means simply 'recently'. It may be, however, that the writer's choice of this word is influenced by the description of the Temple 'so recently purified' after desecration under Antiochus Epiphanes, mentioned in II Macc. 14.36, and a similar reference in Judith 4.3 – both in passages which have much in common with Hebrews. The rededication of the Temple was regularly celebrated by New Testament times, as it still is by Jews as the festival of Hanukkah. The use of another unusual word, translated *inaugurated* in 9.18, perhaps better than *opened* here, suggests the same idea of solemn dedication. (The corresponding noun, 'encaenia', used of Hanukkah in John 10.22, is still used at Oxford University as the name of an annual commemoration ceremony.)

10.21   recalls 3.1-6, which argued that Christ, unlike Moses, was set by God *over* his *household* or people. This thought is combined, as in 3.1, with Jesus' title of *great* or *high priest*.

All this refers to what Christ has done, and thus to resources already available to Christians. *10.22-25* encourages the readers to take full advantage of it, and describes the way of life appropriate to those whose way to God is now open.

Let us make our approach uses Hebrews' usual verb (translated *come* in 12.18-22) for approaching God in worship. Here as often the writer places himself alongside his readers, using 'we' forms here and generally in the following verses (even the warning in v. 26! – but see comment on 'we see' in v. 25). The *blood of the covenant* in v. 29 is not to be sharply distinguished from Jesus' *flesh* in v. 20, or his *body* in v. 10: all three expressions, depending on the context, may refer to his sacrificial death. *In sincerity of heart* is literally 'with true hearts', 'true' meaning purified from sin, and perhaps also faithful. *Full assurance of faith* is close to the 'full assurance of hope' (RSV) mentioned in 6.11, and the *confession of our hope* in v. 23. As chapter 11 will show, faith in Hebrews normally looks forward. *Inwardly cleansed* brings out the meaning of what is literally 'washed [as to] the hearts.' Reference to the 'conscience' confirms this. *Outwardly washed* (literally, 'washed as to the body') 'with pure water' seems to refer to Christian baptism. In Western church history overemphasis on the outward sign in Roman Catholic circles has sometimes led Protestants to undervalue it; but in Hebrews, as in John 3.5, the sign and the reality are not contrasted but bound together. The words for *cleansed* and *washed* indicate lasting states.

10.23   expresses the whole purpose of Hebrews: compare 4.14 (*let us hold fast to the faith we profess*); 3.5f. (*faithful*); 6.13-20 (on the reliability of God's promise).

10.24f.   turn from the readers' relationship with God to their relationship with one another. The writer has never said that he fears the whole community will abandon its faith; rather that certain members will become detached from it and fall away. We do not know whether these are the same people who *stay away from our* *meetings*; but one defence against loss of faith is the practical one of Christian fellowship, about which the writer will have more to say in 13.10–15.

Love, for Paul and John, is God's undemanding self-giving to humanity, reflected in believers' self-giving to God and to one another; it is a distinctively Christian word. Hebrews, like the synoptic gospels, does not use it much; here it is linked with work, that is, *service* (6.10) or *active goodness* (literally, 'good works'; *all goodness* in 13.21 is literally 'every good work'). Unlike Paul, the writer of Hebrews does not seem to have felt it necessary to warn his readers against trying to earn salvation by good deeds. Even Paul (not only in the Pastorals) often speaks about the need for good actions as the fruit of Christian living (see Rom. 2.7; 13.3; II Cor. 9.8; Eph. 2.10; Phil. 1.6; Col. 1.10; II Thess. 2.17). Hebrews is however closer to James in linking faith and love with active goodness (see James 2.8, 14–26).

Arouse in v. 24, the Greek form of our word 'paroxysm', expresses strong emotion; its only other use in the New Testament is of the *dispute* between Paul and Barnabas in Acts 15.39. In the present version the emotion is positive; its purpose, like that of the writer of Hebrews, is to *encourage* (v. 25; compare 13.22). Yet one can imagine that if the readers took Hebrews' appeals and warnings as a model for the way in which they addressed one another, the result could have been something more bracing than the superficial consensus which characterizes the life of some Christian communities today.

The tone of v. 25 prepares for the warning in the following verses. Even the word which is correctly translated *encourage* has a range of meaning which includes strenuous and urgent appeal. This is so here; for the time is short.

This thought runs right through the New Testament, and constitutes one of its greatest unsolved problems. Some sayings attributed to Jesus suggest that the end, the day of the Lord, or the final judgment, is coming soon (see for example Mark 9.1 and parallels; 13.29f. and parallels). Paul even had to warn the Christians of Thessaloniki against rumours that the day of the Lord had already come (II Thess. 2.2). He could himself write to the Romans (13.11) that *deliverance*, that is, final salvation (compare Heb. 9.28) 'is nearer to us now than it was when first we believed'. By the time II Peter was written, perhaps early in the second century, 'scoffers' were asking: 'What has happened to his promised coming?' (3.3f.).

The end of Heb. 10.25 is literally, 'you see the day approach.' REB's *we see* seems to be a mistake for 'you see', as in other translations including NEB. The meaning of the expression 'the day' is well brought out in *the day of the Lord*. The writer seems to think of it primarily as a day of judgment.

The question why the first two generations of Christians seem to have expected that history would soon come to an end is too large to be settled in a short commentary on Hebrews. The most likely explanation may be that they were so convinced that the coming of Christ was *the climax of history* (Heb. 9.26) that they could see little left to happen. With hindsight, we may think that they misinterpreted the ultimacy of the Christ-event in chronological terms, as something happening, not only as the completion of God's purpose for humanity, but also at the end of time. Opinions not surprisingly differ, and we cannot be sure.

The warning passage *10.26–31* reinforces and complements that in *6.4f.* The distinction between deliberate and unintentional sin is clearly made in Num. 15.22–31; even under the old covenant they were to be dealt with differently. Deliberate (*presumptuous*) sin is defined as 'insulting the LORD' and 'bringing the word of the LORD into contempt' (vv. 30f). Those who commit such sins are to be 'cut off from the people' (v.30). What this might mean in practice is shown by the story, told immediately after, of a man whom God commanded to be stoned to death for gathering sticks on the sabbath (vv. 32–36).

It is reasonable to suppose that the writer of Hebrews has this passage in mind as he refers in v. 26 to deliberate sin among Christians. It is more difficult to tell how far he supposes the distinction between deliberate and unintentional sin to have been affected by the change from the old to the new covenant. Certain points at least are clear. (1) The writer's thought is now moving into an area where no sacrifices is effective. Under the old order, this was because no sacrifice was prescribed, but only the death penalty. Under the new order, it is because after Christ *there can be no further sacrifice for sins*. (2) The old and the new order are now compared rather than contrasted, in a 'how much more' argument (vv. 28f.) strongly reminiscent of 2.2f., but stronger. (3) The deliberate sin, whatever it is, is not a single act, but either a series of repeated acts, or a continuous state of 'persist[ing] in sin'; GNB 'go on sinning'. In the light of 6.4ff., it is natural to think of this sin as apostasy, a wilful and permanent rejection of the truth once seen and accepted in Christ.

Receiving the knowledge of the truth may refer, like v. 22, to baptism, by implication of adults. If this is so we have here an early form of the later teaching that baptism left an indelible mark on those who received it; they could never be the same again.

The word for *knowledge* is a (possibly stronger) compound of the normal Greek word for knowledge, which is 'gnosis'. The writer of Hebrews never uses the simple form, perhaps because it was already coming to be used by those, later known as 'gnostics', who claimed special secret knowledge of supernatural matters. The writer similarly avoids other such terms, such as 'light' and 'mystery'; but unlike Paul (for example I Cor. 8.1–3; Col. 2.8), he does not directly attack those who claim this secret knowledge.

10.27 describes God's judgment in language similar to that of the Septuagint Greek version of Isa. 23.11. There, as in the present verse, a word meaning 'adversaries' is used; not the more common word for *enemies* which the writer of Hebrews (not a polemical writer) uses only in quoting Ps. 110.1 (Heb. 1.13; 10.13). *God's* is implied, as in the Greek of Isa. 26.11.

10.28 refers to a rule of evidence laid down in Deut. 17.6; 19.15. The writer of Hebrews is only interested in the punishment; the point in Deuteronomy was that the death penalty must not be imposed on the evidence of a single witness. The words *without mercy* are taken from Deut. 19.21. Here, Hebrews is closer to the meaning of the Old Testament text: in both places, implicitly in Hebrews and explicitly in Deuteronomy, the aim is to keep God's people holy. (Deut. 19 also discusses the distinction between accidental and deliberate homicide.) The writer of Hebrews may also have been influenced and encouraged by the Old Testament context. His own purpose, in the present passage, is well described in Deut. 19.20: 'The rest of the people when they hear of it will be afraid, and never again will anything as wicked as this be done among you.'

10.29 What punishment, one might ask, can be worse than death? The writer does not say, preferring to concentrate on describing in greater detail the significance of the sin, and leaving its punishment with God. This verse is probably a rhetorical question: 'What, then, of the person who despises the Son of God?' (GNB); REB understands it as an emphatic statement.

Most translations agree with REB in translating *will be deserved*. Alternatively, the meaning may be 'will be considered worthy', that is, by God; NJB 'will be condemned'. *Trampled underfoot* is used figuratively to express extreme contempt, as for example in the Greek of Zech. 12.3: 'every one who tramples on [Jerusalem] shall utterly mock at it.' In using the solemn title *the Son of God*, the writer of Hebrews recalls what was said earlier, especially in ch. 1, about the supremacy of the Son. To *profane* means to treat as ordinary something which has been set apart for God; GNB 'treats as a cheap thing'. *The blood of the covenant* recalls Ex. 24.8, quoted in Heb. 9.20; but here it means the new covenant in Christ's blood, by which believers have themselves been *consecrated* (10.10) or set apart for God. *God's gracious Spirit*, literally 'the Spirit of grace', may mean the Spirit whom God gives, or the Spirit through whom God gives his gifts (compare *the heavenly gift* in 6.4; also Luke 11.13; John 3.34; I Thess. 4.8). All this is either traditional teaching or teaching which has been given in detail earlier in Hebrews. If the readers ignore it there is no hope for them.

This passage is a good example of the way in which the writer develops a theme with ever greater force. He did it with his treatment of Old Testament sacrifices, leading progressively up to the statement in 10.9 that they had been 'abolished'. So here in his approach to those whom he feared to be in spiritual danger. Earlier, he has described them comparatively gently as *slow to learn* (5.11) or *lax* (6.12); their danger was described as *drifting* (2.1) or 'ignor[ing]' (2.3). Now the real nature of their danger is described in the strongest possible terms as deliberate and persistent revolt against God, rejection of all that he has done for them in Christ.

10.30   The argument is confirmed by quotation of two lines from Deut. 32.35f. which speak of God as judge. The first of these is also quoted in Rom. 12.19. Exceptionally for Hebrews, the wording is closer to the Hebrew than to the Greek; perhaps the text circulated independently as a popular saying. Paul uses the text to argue that Christians should not seek revenge themselves but leave it to God; Hebrews is closer to the spirit of Deut. 32.

The second quotation is also found in Ps. 135.14, but it is natural to suppose that the writer of Hebrews took both lines from the same passage.

10.31   rounds off the warning with a statement which the readers were not likely to question. Fear is a rather frequent theme in Hebrews (see v. 27; 2.15; 4.1; 12.21); but so is fearlessness (13.6 = Ps. 118.6), especially in Old Testament characters (11.23,27). As the writer has already said, if salvation, from one point of view, is *to serve the living*

God (9.14), there is nothing worse than to prove a *deserter* from him (3.12).

10.32–39 From warning, the writer turns gradually to encouragement, on the basis of the readers' past record. He followed the same course in 6.10, after the warning of 6.4–6. Their early days as Christians had been marked by suffering, intense struggle, and endurance: the endurance which the writer wants his readers to maintain to the end (3.6,14).

The word for *struggle* is used outside the Bible of athletic contests. This metaphor will return more strongly in 12.1. It is one of the links between the end of ch. 10 and the beginning of ch. 12 which have led some to think of ch. 11 as a deviation, perhaps a separate sermon by the same author. There are, however, also links between chs. 10 and 11, notably the mention of faith in 10.38f.

10.33f. In its early days, the community had stood together, whether its members were personally attacked or not. Verse 34 specifies in what the persecution consisted, while the first part of v. 33 speaks rather of the effect of the persecutions. The word for *publicly exposed* is related to the word 'theatre', and suggests being made a public spectacle. The word for *tormented* suggests constricting pressure. This is its only occurrence in Hebrews, but other New Testament writers, especially Paul, use it often as a general term for persecution.

These sufferings had been accepted *cheerfully*, literally, 'with joy' (NJB, similarly RSV, NIV). Joy, not only despite but in and even because of suffering, seems to have been a distinctive characteristic of the first Christians. The theme of joy in suffering is perhaps developed most fully in I Peter, who describes Christians as sharing in Christ's sufferings (4.13; compare 1.6,8; 3.14). This teaching may even go back to Jesus' words '*Blessed*' (or 'happy', GNB) 'are those who are persecuted in the cause of right' (Matt. 5.10). Hebrews similarly speaks of Christ enduring the cross *for the sake of the joy that lay ahead of him* (12.2; compare 13.17).

In the present verse, however, the contrast is between the loss of earthly possessions and the sure hope of *a better, more lasting possession* in heaven. This is a fairly common thought. The writer may be thinking, as in 11.13–16, of the heavenly counterpart of the promised land; or of Jews' sufferings in the time of the Maccabees (for example, II Macc. 6–7); or of Jesus' saying about treasure in heaven (Matt. 6.19f.).

Knowing that you had is not very clear in English; 'knowing that you still possessed something much better, which would last forever' (GNB) is clearer. The word translated *had* suggests present and continuous possession.

10.35 Encouragement rather than warning continues to be the dominant note. *Confidence* is a word translated *fearless* in 3.6, on which see the comment. In the present verse, it seems to indicate primarily confidence in the face of persecution; but confidence in approaching God through Christ may also be implied.

The *reward* is doubtless the future aspect of the present and continuous possession of which v. 34 spoke, and on which Moses' eyes are said in 11.26 to have been fixed. For Hebrews, expectation of a reward is an integral part of a belief in God which is not theoretical but living (11.6). Jesus also spoke freely of rewards (see, for example, Matt. 5.12 and parallel; Mark 9.41 and parallel), and so did Paul (I Cor. 3.8,14; 9.17f.). Paul was aware of the danger of misunderstanding this teaching as justification by works (Rom. 4.4–8); but in the present verse, and elsewhere, a reward in heaven is assumed to be a gift from God.

10.36 continues and reinforces the same theme. REB correctly translates *you need*, because endurance is an essential condition; the word sometimes means 'you lack'. The end of the Christian life, like the end of Jesus' own earthly life (10.5–10), is to align one's own will with that of God.

10.37 The mention in v. 36 of *what* God *has promised* points forward to the quotation of a promise from Scripture. Yet paradoxically, just as the promise of the new covenant was introduced in 8.8 by a mention of 'God finding fault with his people', so conversely here a rather threatening quotation is introduced as a promise. The reason for this will become clear in v. 39.

The quotation is mostly from Hab. 2.3f., quoted basically from the Greek as usual, but with some changes (see below). The words *very soon*, however, come from Isa. 26.20 ('a little while'); the wording is more distinctive than it sounds in English. This is a chapter which the writer of Hebrews had in mind in 10.27 (compare Isa. 26.11). *Very soon* expresses once more to the writer's expectation of *the day of the Lord drawing near* (see comment on Heb. 10.25).

The writer makes various changes to his Greek Old Testament text which, though small in themselves, add up to a substantial change in meaning. Where Habbakuk spoke of a vision to come, Hebrews says: *he who is to come*. Where Habbakuk says that the vision 'will not delay' (RSV), Hebrews applies these words to the one who is to come. The order of the clauses quoted in v. 38 is reversed, and there are other minor changes.

The writer of Hebrews applies the first part of the quotation to Christ and his expected return, and the second part to members of God's people, who are further divided into those who remain faithful and those who do not. *My righteous servant*, literally, 'my righteous one', refers to anyone who is righteous, that is, who does God's will.

Despite the changes of wording in Hebrews, and the fresh application, Hebrews' understanding of Habbakuk is probably closer to the text than Paul's. Paul quotes one line of the passage, in Rom. 1.17 and Gal. 3.11, to mean 'anyone who is righteous, not by works but by faith, will live.' Habbakuk, like Hebrews, is saying that God will protect anyone who remains faithful to him in a crisis which is coming.

10.39   The latter part of the quotation has distinguished between two groups of people. The writer now expresses his confidence that, despite all his fears and warnings, 'we' (emphatic) belong, not to the group who are 'lost' or 'destroyed' (NIV), but to the group who keep faith. Chapter 11 will speak of other members of that great and noble band, and end (11.40) by linking them once more with the writer and his readers.

11.1–40   *Faith in times past*

Israel is known as a people of the book, and that book is essentially a book of history. It is therefore not surprising that ancient Jewish and Christian writings should contain a number of retellings of Israel's history, each having a particular end in view. In addition to the present chapter, the biblical retellings include the following:

(1) Some of the Psalms were a means of handing on historical tradition, first orally and then in writing (see Ps. 44.1ff.; 78.1–6). For example, Ps. 78 retells the exodus story, emphasizing, in the same spirit as Heb. 3.7 – 4.13, the need to avoid Israel's bad example, but ending with a reference to David and to the centralization of worship in Jerusalem. In Ps. 105 the stress is rather on God's faithfulness in

delivering his covenant people from slavery in Egypt. Ps. 106 similarly concentrates on the exodus, but also mentions how God rescued his people on later occasions (vv. 40–46).

(2) Wisdom. 10 interprets history from Adam to the exodus as the story of God's people guided and supported by wisdom. Individuals are not named, but some translations identify them in section headings (GNB) or footnotes (NJB).

(3) Ecclus. (Ben Sira) 44–50 is the well-known passage beginning 'Let us now praise famous men'; the Hebrew text has 'godly' (GNB). The writer reviews Israelite history from Enoch to Solomon. He lays particular stress on the priestly figures Aaron (45.6–22), Phinehas (vv. 23–26), and the reigning high priest Simon, son of Onias (50.1–21), none of whom is mentioned in Heb. 11. He pays much more attention than Hebrews to the kings of Israel, condemning not only Rehoboam and Jeroboam (47.23f.), but also Solomon (47. 12–22), despite his wisdom. He also lays stress on God's repeated covenants with his people from Noah to David, but the brief note on Jeremiah (49.7) does not mention his prophecy of a new covenant.

(4) The Books of the Maccabees contain various shorter summaries of Israel's history. In I Macc. 2.49–60, Mattathias reminds his sons of earlier generations, from Abraham to Daniel, who had defended God's covenant; he encourages his sons to follow these examples (vv. 61–64); and he commends, together with them, his own sons Simon and Judas Maccabaeus (vv. 65f.). Among the non-canonical writings, Simon's prayer in III Macc. 2.2–20 contains several references to victories which show how God judges 'all who act with pride and insolence' (v . 3). (A nearby passage, III Macc. 1.11, refers to the rule that only the high priest could enter the inner sanctuary, and he only once a year.) The priest Eleazar's prayer in III Macc. 6.16–23 similarly mentions how God had given victory to his people on various occasions from the exodus to the time of Daniel. In IV Macc. 16.16–23 Eleazar's wife encourages her sons by the example of Abraham's willingness to sacrifice Isaac, and by God's deliverance of Daniel and his companions.

(5) The closest New Testament parallel to Heb. 11 is no doubt Stephen's speech in Acts 7. Yet on closer comparison, the differences between these two chapters come to seem more striking than the points of contact, which will be noted in the comments on individual verses below. Stephen covers the period from Abraham to Solomon, but his story is one not of faith, but of the people's disobedience to God. The tone is thus much more polemical than anything in Hebrews. Stephen is replying to his attackers, perhaps knowing

already that he has nothing to lose, whereas the writer of Hebrews is trying to persuade his friends, for whom he has much to gain. In contrast with frequent Old Testament quotations in Stephen's speech, Hebrews 11 surprisingly contains only three quotations (vv. 5, 18, 21), though many other references to Scripture.

Although this chapter thus stands within a long tradition of retellings of Israel's history, there is no reason to doubt that it is by the same author as the rest of Hebrews, or to think that the range of his illustrations is taken from a source other than the Old Testament itself. There is nothing else in Hebrews like it, not even 3.7 – 4.13, but its language and thought are sufficiently similar to the rest of Hebrews for us not to suppose that it was by a different author. The Old Testament examples reinforce the writer's appeal to his readers for endurance in the faith. If (which we cannot know) it originally circulated as a separate sermon, the writer has skilfully welded it with the rest of the letter.

11.1 *Faith* is obviously the key word of this chapter; the importance of faith was already stressed in 4.2f., and just before this chapter in 10.38f.; it will be stressed again in 12.2,7. Jesus is described in 2.17; 3.2 as faithful to God; and God's own faithfulness is recognized in 10.23; 11.11. Faith, in Hebrews, is the positive human response to a message from God. Since that message is often a promise, faith is often shown as forward-looking, and therefore closely linked with hope, as in the present verse. It is also linked with *patience* (6.12) or endurance; it involves holding on to Christ to the end. Hebrews does not speak of 'the faith' in the sense of a body of teaching: his word for that is literally 'confession', translated in 3.1 as *the faith we profess*. Unlike Paul, Hebrews does not describe faith as intense mystical communion with Christ; indeed, he often does not specify whether the faith is in God or in Christ.

11.1 is less a definition of faith than a description of what faith does; a description filled out by the chapter as a whole.

The word translated *substance* has various senses, all more or less closely connected with the idea of stability, an idea which also underlies the Hebrew words for faith. The most likely meaning here is simply that of 'being sure' (NIV, similarly GNB); NJB's 'guarantee' rightly suggests that there is reason to be sure.

On their own, the words *realities we do not see* suggest another reference to the distinction between the earthly and heavenly worlds, as for example in 9.23 and 11.3. It is also possible to see, here as in the first half of the verse, a reference to the *unseen future* which will be mentioned in v. 7. Believers do not see these heavenly realities yet, but they soon will if they hold firm.

11.2 introduces the series of Old Testament examples. *For their faith* (also NJB) may be translated 'by their faith' (GNB similarly RSV; NRSV has 'by faith', with a note reading 'Gk *by this*'). The word translated *won God's approval*, literally 'were witnessed to,' refers to the testimony of God in Scripture.

11.3 After the words *by faith we understand*, the rest of the verse largely says the same thing twice for emphasis. God's command, 'Let there be . . .' (Gen. 1.3 etc.) comes from the invisible world, and brings the visible universe into being. It is by their faith that believers recognize God as creator. Paul in Rom. 1.20 draws the further consequence that people are inexcusable if they do not recognize God in the visible universe.

11.4 Compare Gen. 4.1–16, especially v. 4. The Genesis story does not say why God accepted Abel's sacrifice and rejected Cain's. Hebrews contains by implication two interlocking arguments:

1.1 God was pleased with Abel.
1.2 'Without faith it is impossible to please him' (11.6).
1.3 Therefore Abel must have had faith.

2.1 Faith is closely linked with righteousness (10.38).
2.2 Abel had faith (point 1.3).
2.3 Therefore Abel must have been a righteous man. (The word for 'goodness' here is the same as that translated *righteous* in 10.38).

The last point is not directly *attested* in Scripture, but the writer does not expect his readers to question it.

There is no difference of meaning in Hebrews between animal *sacrifice* and the word for *offerings*, often used of cereal offerings. Abel's offering in any case was a firstborn animal (Gen. 4.2).

The surprising statement that Abel *continues to speak* is based on the present tense used in Gen. 4.10, where God says: 'Your brother's blood is crying out to me from the ground.' Scripture, as the word of God, has for the writer of Hebrews an indestructible life (compare 4.12f.). This makes it possible for him to draw from it new meanings and applications for his own generation.

11.5 There was an immense amount of speculation about Enoch in ancient times, but the writer of Hebrews argues essentially from the basic text, Gen. 5.24f, which reads: 'Enoch walked with God and then was seen no more, because God had taken him away'. Compare also Ecclus. (Ben Sira) 44.10; Wisd. 4.16. The phrase which in Hebrew means 'he walked with God' is translated in the Greek Old Testament as 'he pleased God'. First the writer of Hebrews introduces the text in his own words; then he quotes and briefly comments on the two parts of the text, in reverse order. This emphasizes the fact that Enoch *pleased God*, and lays the basis for *11.6* which argues (1) that Enoch must therefore have had faith, and (2) that this applies to worshippers generally. *Comes to God* is a frequent expression in Hebrews (see comment on 4.16) for approaching God in worship. Belief in God's existence is fundamental, indeed elementary (see 6.1–2), but more is needed: belief that he is a living God who *rewards those who seek him* (see comment on 10.35).

The verb translated *was taken up*, and the corresponding noun translated *was taken*, mean removal from one place to another; the same verb is translated 'removed' in Acts 7.16. *Up to another life* is implied.

Mention of Enoch raises to a lesser extent the kind of questions which surround Melchizedek in ch. 7. Melchizedek was the first priest mentioned in Scripture, and Enoch is the first of whom it is said that he *was taken up to another life without passing through death*. We do not know how the writer of Hebrews would have answered the objection that this was the prerogative of Christ, as 'first fruits of the harvest of the dead' (I Cor. 15.20). The Christian author of the *Ascension of Isaiah* 9.9–18 (perhaps second century CE) recalls Heb. 11.39 by speaking of Enoch as one of those who do not yet possess their thrones or crowns, since the righteous have not yet ascended with Christ. See also comment on 11.37.

11.7   The story of Noah in Gen. 6–9 says nothing about his faith, but it does state that Noah pleased God (6.9), for which the writer has just said that faith is a condition. There is little in common between what Hebrews says about Noah and what is said in I Peter 3.20 and II Peter 2.5.

REB rearranges the sentence in translation; RSV and NIV offer more literal versions. The word translated *took good heed* may refer either (1) to fear, (2) to prudence, as in Gen. 6–9, or (3) to reverence for God. (1) is difficult to reconcile with faith. (3) is probably the meaning here. 'Divine' is implied. *Warning* may also include instructions for building the ark. *The unseen future* is literally 'things not yet seen'. The boat called an *ark* has nothing to do with the holy box called the Ark of the Testimony, for example in Ex. 25.16; 26.33f., and the Ark of the Covenant of the LORD in Num. 10.33; 14.44 and elsewhere – except that both were associated with a covenant between God and his people (Gen. 6.18). *Save* here involves physical rescue, not spiritual deliverance as for example in Heb. 2.3, though I Peter 3.20f. sees Noah's ark as a symbol of 'baptism, through which you are now brought to safety'.

Noah's faith made him listen to what God told him , and do what God said. His faith was thus forward-looking, anticipating the disaster of the flood, and following God's instructions on how to meet it. It is not quite clear why Noah is said to have *put the whole world in the wrong*, literally, 'judged the world'. Other writers speak of Noah as a preacher of righteousness, and this may be the meaning here. More probably, his example, as 'the one blameless man of his time' (Gen. 6.9) showed up by contrast his contemporaries' wickedness, and silently passed judgment on it. *Made good his claim to the righteousness which comes of faith* is literally 'became an heir of the righteousness [which is] according to faith.' In fact, Noah was called righteous before he received and fulfilled God's commission to build the ark. After the flood God grants to Noah, as the head of the sole surviving family, the authority over creation which he had originally given to Adam (compare Gen. 1.28–30 and 9.1–3). The writer of Hebrews may therefore mean here that God gave Noah a reward appropriate to someone who is righteous by faith. Most translations, however, think of God's gift to Noah as that of righteousness itself; 'Noah received from God the righteousness that comes from faith' (GNB). At this point, exceptionally, Hebrews sounds like Paul; but the wording is more simply explained by the influence of Hab. 2.3f., quoted in Heb. 10.37f.

11.8–19   In Hebrews Abraham and Moses are the two most prominent Old Testament figures. Both are subordinated to Christ, Moses in 3.1–6 and Abraham in 7.1–10; yet Abraham is honoured as the one to whom God has promised that he would become the father of many nations (6.13f., compare comment on 2.16). Here, as elsewhere in ch. 11, the idea of being lower than Christ is not restated. The incompleteness of the old order is shown in a different way, by taking the story of Abraham and Sarah as an example of how God's promises may be fulfilled on an earthly level, but still leave something to hope for.

If these verses are read in this light, the problem of the apparent interruption of the story in vv. 13–16 disappears. On one level, the story is one of faith in God's promises triumphing over great obstacles: a journey without a destination (v. 8), life as an alien in a then foreign land (v. 9), and (the greatest test of all) the sacrifice of Isaac, through whom Abraham's *countless* descendants were to be traced (vv. 17f.). On this level the story is complete in itself: the hardships and dangers are overcome, and in due course, as the readers well know, the promised land is occupied.

But it is essential to the argument of Hebrews to show that the story has another, eternal dimension. The history as told in Genesis (especially chs. 12 and 22) is not dissolved into allegory, but it points to something greater. This further dimension is first mentioned in v. 10, and then developed in vv. 13–16. Verse 10 refers only to Abraham; vv. 13–16 include all the Old Testament figures mentioned so far in chapter 11. The implied conclusion is that faith looks not only forwards but upwards.

11.8   recalls Gen. 12.1–5 (compare Acts 7.2ff.). *Leave his home* and *went away* translate the same verb, literally 'go out' (that is, from Abraham's home country, Harran). The repetition of the verb points up the contrast between past and future, between God's sure promise of the land and his human insecurity. The same verb will be used again in the final appeal (13.13).

The between past and future contrast is sharpened still further in *11.9*. Abraham and his family were actually living in the land which God had promised them; yet their present state was that of nomadic aliens.

For Abraham to have been living *with Isaac and Jacob* is difficult to reconcile with the dating of events in Genesis (see especially 26.1). Yet that is what the Greek means, and RSV, REB, and NJB are right, over against 'as did Isaac and Jacob' in NEB, NIV and later editions of GNB. As in his description of the tabernacle, the writer of Hebrews is not always concerned with accuracy in insignificant details.

11.10   The significance of the paradox is now explained. Even in the earthly promised land, Abraham and his family lived as aliens, because they knew that Canaan was not their ultimate destination. Why else, the writer might ask, should they have behaved in such a contradictory manner? Abraham's faith is seen in his ability to look even beyond God's literal keeping of his promises to fulfilment in God himself, the maker not only of earth but of heaven (compare 1.10–12; 3.4; 8.2).

A city with firm foundations is literally 'the city having the foundations'. On one level this is a contrast with tents, which have no foundations. On another level, as the following words make plain, it is a contrast between the heavenly city and anything built by human hands (compare 12.26–28). *Architect* is the word used for God in Wisd. 13.1, and translated *artificer*; the feminine form is used of divine wisdom *whose skill made all things*, in Wisd. 7.22; compare 8.6; 14.2. *Builder* is used of human workmen, especially makers of idols in Acts 19.24, 38; Rev. 18.22; it is appropriately used here in a good sense of God.

11.12   Sarah, like other members of Abraham's family, receives from God a promise which, it seems, is impossible even for God to fulfil. Strictly speaking, the promise is made to Abraham in Sarah's hearing (Gen. 17.19; 10.11–14; compare 21.2). The only time the Lord speaks directly to Sarah, it is to insist that she laughed at the idea that she could become a mother (18.15) – scarcely an attitude which suggests faith!

Before tackling this problem, however, it is necessary to try to find out exactly what the author of Hebrews wrote: because the manuscripts vary, and the meaning is uncertain. The main options are as follows:

(1) 'By faith Sarah herself also received power to conceive . . .' (RSV, similarly REB, NJB). The problem is that the word translated 'power to conceive' does not have this meaning elsewhere; it was always used at this time of a man's power to beget children.

(2) 'It was faith that made Abraham able to become a father . . .' (GNB, similarly NIV). This avoids the problems of (1), but leaves the meaning of the reference to Sarah uncertain. (a) It may be an aside: '(and Sarah herself was barren)' (NIV, similarly GNB); or (b) it may mean 'together with Sarah', that is, with Sarah's involvement. (b) is chosen by many commentators, and is probably the best option, though major English translations do not adopt it. If it is correct, this verse does not refer directly to Sarah's faith, and there is no contradiction or tension with the picture of Sarah in Gen. 18.11–14. In any case, both Abraham and Sarah began by finding the Lord's promise of a son difficult to credit.

11.12   Several Old Testament passages contrast Israel's small beginnings with its later prosperity; for example:

Consider Abraham your father

and Sarah who gave you birth:
when I called him he was but one;
I blessed him and made him many

(Isa. 51.2; compare Deut. 26.5).

As good as dead implies 'too old to beget children'. The rest of the verse, beautiful in both rhythm and imagery, recalls Gen. 22.17; 32.12; Ex. 32.13; Deut. 1.10; 3.36 LXX; 10.22. *Countless* recalls the Lord's words to Abram in Gen. 15.5: 'Look up at the sky, and count the stars, if you can. So many will your descendants be.' This is immediately followed by the statement: 'Abram put his faith in the LORD, who reckoned it to him as righteousness' (Gen. 15.6, quoted in Rom. 4.3, 9, 22; Gal. 3.6; James 2.23), which was probably in the mind of the writer of Hebrews also.

11.13f. This and the following verses are central to both the structure and the meaning of chapter 11. *All these* is most naturally taken to refer back to people already mentioned. But there is another *all these* in v. 39, including all the Old Testament figures mentioned. There are more similarities than differences between the smaller and the larger group. True, the later generations did not share in the patriarchs' nomadic life on earth; but, in the sense which ultimately matters most for the writer of Hebrews, they too *were longing for a better country* (v. 15) which they *did not receive* (v. 39).

How does the writer know this? From Scripture. *Strangers and aliens without fixed abode on earth* translates a phrase found in slightly different forms in Gen. 23.4; 47.9; I Chron. 29.15; Ps. 39.12; compare I Peter 2.11. Just as in Heb. 7.3 the writer drew conclusions from what Scripture did not say about Melchizedek, so here he deduces from the fact that the patriarchs had no *fixed abode on earth* the conclusion that they must have been looking for one in heaven. The words *on earth* are emphasized.

11.15 More precisely, although they were actually in the promised land, the patriarchs went on living like people who had not reached their destination, but were *looking for a country of their own*. The word translated *a country of their own* normally means 'a fatherland', 'a native country'. But the point is precisely that this country for which they were looking must have been different from their place of origin. They did not need to 'look' for that: they knew the way back there, and nothing was preventing them from taking that road.

11.16 *Instead*, Scripture shows them insisting that they are landless nomads on earth, therefore by implication that their true destination is heaven. *We find them longing for a better country* is literally 'they long for a better country'; the present tense is used to refer to the permanent record of Scripture.

Their longing is not in vain: God has in fact prepared for believers *a city*; by definition, since God himself has built it (v. 10), a heavenly city (compare Rev. 21). They have not yet taken possession of it (Heb. 11.39f.), but it is there waiting for them, like God's 'place of rest' in 3.7 – 4.13. The thought is similar to John 14.1–4, though the language and setting are different. Both John 14 and the present passage, however, may well have been written for the encouragement of early Christian groups subject to similar pressures on their faith.

By building this heavenly city for his people God has committed himself to them in the covenant loyalty of which Hebrews spoke earlier, especially in 9.15–22. A negative way of expressing the same thought is to say that he *is not ashamed* of his people. Among many peoples shame is a more powerful concept than sin. Although this is not true in the Hebrew and Christian tradition, the theme of shame runs strongly through the Bible. The second part of the present verse probably implies: 'The reason why God (in Ex. 3.6; compare Gen. 28.13) allows himself to be identified as "the God of Abraham, Isaac, and Jacob" is that he has committed himself to his people by already preparing for them the heavenly city which they sought by faith during their earthly lives.' In the same way, Christ now in heaven identifies himself with *his brothers* (12.11); compare Mark 8.36 and parallels; II Tim. 1.8. Conversely, in the description of Moses (Heb. 11.23–27), faith is closely linked with the rejection of high earthly status, and with accepting the *stigma that rests on God's Anointed*; compare 13.13.

11.17f.   Verse 17 essentially says the same thing twice for emphasis; and for good measure, v. 18 quotes the promise referred to in the second part of v. 17. God's test or trial of Abraham (Gen. 22.1–10; compare James 2.21) places him in an even more paradoxical situation than the one mentioned in Heb. 11.9. God had promised that Abraham would have countless descendants (v. 12) through Isaac; yet now God asks Abraham to kill Isaac as a sacrifice! This was surely a supreme test of faith: yet Abraham does not hesitate. The writer of Hebrews does not need to remind his readers that at the last moment God provided an animal sacrifice as a substitute. The point is that Abraham was ready to do what God had asked, however irrational his demands might seem.

One of the most profound reinterpretations of the story of Abraham and Isaac is Søren Kierkegaard's *Fear and Trembling*.[1] Anyone studying Hebrews alongside Kierkegaard may like to compare Kierkegaard's definition of faith with Hebrews', and the relative importance of the individual and the people of God in Kierkegaard and in the biblical accounts (Gen. 22 and Hebrews).

The word which is correctly translated *put to the test* also means 'tempted'. It is in this sense that James 1.13 says: 'God does not himself tempt anyone,' that is, to do wrong. The use of the word 'tempt' in Gen 22.1 puzzled ancient commentators, but there is no problem if it is recognized that the word has two quite different meanings, depending on the context.

In fact, Isaac was not Abraham's only son; but Hebrews, following Jewish tradition, does not count Ishmael (Gen. 15.16) as a child of promise. Paul makes the same point explicitly in Rom. 9.7f.

Hebrews does not distinguish between the *promises* in v. 17 and the one promise quoted from Gen. 21.12 in v. 18. The same promise of descendants was made repeatedly to the patriarchs. Paul refers in the same general way to *the promises* in Rom. 9.4. There is however no reason to think that the writer of Hebrews had read Rom. 9, or *vice versa*. The gradual, painful split between Judaism and Christianity marks almost all New Testament writings in different ways (see especially Rom. 9. 1–5).

11.19 This verse has no direct Old Testament basis. In the first part the writer suggests how Abraham might have resolved the paradox of God's demand for the sacrifice of Isaac. In the second part he points to the wider significance of this event. The words rather weakly translated *in a sense* ('figuratively speaking' RSV, NIV, NJB; 'so to speak', GNB) were translated 'symbolically' in 9.9. Isaac's last-minute rescue from the fire prefigures the resurrection of Christians; but the reality of that resurrection is still to come.

11.20 A generation later, Isaac's blessing of Jacob and Esau (Gen. 27.27ff., 39f.) is another example of forward-looking faith. Through the unedifying story of Jacob deceiving his father and elder brother God's purposes for his chosen people Israel are carried forward. The writer of Hebrews passes lightly over this episode, but cannot omit it altogether, since it is an essential link in God's dealings with

---

[1] 1843; English translation by A. Hannay, Harmondsworth: Penguin Books 1985.

Abraham, Isaac and Jacob. *Spoke of things to come* is very general. Hebrews shows no interest in the actual words in which Isaac blesses Jacob. It is enough that the blessing looks to the future of God's people, which the writer sees (Heb. 11.39f.) as having come to fulfilment in Christ.

11.21 From Jacob the line goes on through his twelve sons, the founders of the twelve tribes of Israel (Gen. 48.15f.; 49). *Bowed in worship over the top of his staff* quotes Gen. 47.31 from the Greek; the Hebrew means 'bowed in worship by the head of his bed'. The Hebrew words for 'staff' and 'bed' are very similar, and a Greek translator probably confused them. Once again faith is shown by looking confidently to the future, in which God's purpose will be worked out.

11.22 Hebrews summarizes Gen. 50.24f.: 'God will not fail to come to your aid and take you from here to the land which he promised on oath to Abraham, Isaac, and Jacob.' As a sign of Joseph's confidence in God's purpose for his people, he 'made the sons of Israel' (that is, his own brothers) 'solemnly swear that when God came to their aid, they would carry his bones up with them from there' (that is, from Egypt into the promised land). This conclusion to the book of Genesis thus points directly forward to the exodus; but for the writer of Hebrews it points further forward to God's people in his own time. Compare Ex. 13.19.

11.23–31 In these verses the writer speaks of Moses and the exodus; a subject of equal importance with the story of Abraham. On one level it is the story of how God's purpose for his people continues to be worked out in later generations, despite repeated danger that the line of succession would be cut off. On another level it is the story of how the leaders of God's people looked forward to a greater fulfilment than the occupation of Canaan. The writer keeps for the end of the chapter (vv. 39f.) the fullest statement of what the story means on this higher level. But within the present passage there are already clear clues: especially *the stigma that rests on God's Anointed* (v.26), *his eyes were fixed on the coming reward* (v. 27) *as one who saw the invisible God* (v. 28). The writer is saying in effect to his readers: 'This is not just ancient history: it is your story too.'

11.23 When Moses' mother Jochebed (Ex. 6.20) 'saw what a fine child he was, she kept him hidden for three months' (2.2), because the king of Egypt had ordered all new-born Hebrew boys to be thrown into the Nile (1.22). Hebrews associates Moses' father Amram (6.20; compare 2.1) with hiding the baby. Ex. 2 does not actually say that the parents were not afraid, but that is how Hebrews interprets their disobedience of Pharaoh's orders. Here as in Heb. 11.27 fearlessness is seen as a sign of faith; God's promise matters more than the king of Egypt's threats.

11.24f.   These two verses state another paradox, which v. 26 will reinforce. Moses has to choose between, on the one hand, identification with the Egyptian royal family, in which he had been brought up; and on the other hand, commitment to Israel, to which he belonged by birth. It is a choice between luxury and hardship. But it is also a choice between commitment to *God's people*, and a way of life which by contrast is described simply as *sin*. No doubt the writer of Hebrews did think of life at Pharaoh's court as sinful; not just immoral, but consistently hostile to Israel, as the whole of Ex. 1 – 15 recounts. But the main point is that for Moses to desert God's people and join its enemies would have been an act of apostasy comparable to that which threatens some of the readers of Hebrews.

Pharaoh is a title held by kings of Egypt. The Pharaoh mentioned in Ex. 1–2 may have been Sety I, who reigned in the early thirteenth century BCE. In Heb. 11.23, 27, he is called simply 'the king'.

Transient ('for a little while', GNB) suggests the contrast between what is earthly and therefore temporary, and what is heavenly and eternal (compare *for a short while*, 2.7, 9; 10.34; 12.26ff.; II Cor. 4.18).

In 11.26   the writer offers his interpretation of Moses' action; there is no direct Old Testament basis for what he says. *The stigma that rests on God's Anointed* echoes Ps. 89.50f., which speaks of the enemies of God's people who 'taunted your anointed king at every step'; compare 69.9. These psalms are often referred to in the New Testament: see especially Mark 15.32, 34 and parallels. The stigma of being Christians is mentioned in Heb. 10.33; 13.12f., and recurs in Matt. 5.11 and parallel; Mark 9.41; I Tim. 4.10; I Peter 4.14. *The stigma that rests on God's Anointed* is literally 'the abuse of the Christ'. It is not clear whether the writer of Hebrews is thinking of the abuse which falls (1) on anyone whom God 'anoints', or chooses for a special purpose; or (2) on Christ himself, with whom Moses so to speak identifies himself in advance; or who is thought of as already alive. Most translations apparently choose (1). NIV's 'disgrace for the sake of Christ' suggests (2). This is probably correct, since the writer of

Hebrews shows no interest in the anointing of rulers in Old Testament times; for him, Christ is the Anointed *par excellence*.

In the Old Testament, *wealth* is often seen as a blessing from God (for example, Gen. 31.1), though wisdom is prized more highly (Prov. 8.18–21). In the New Testament, material wealth is always spoken of negatively (Mark 4.19 and parallels; I Tim. 6.17; James 5.2; Rev. 18.17), while positive references to wealth are always spiritual (as here and frequently in Paul, for example Rom. 2.4; II Cor. 8.2; also Rev. 5.12). Once more the writer refers to this kind of wealth as a *reward* (compare 2.2; 10.35; 11.6).

The word used for Moses' *eyes . . . fixed* suggests looking away from Egypt, by implication to the promised land and ultimately to heaven. A different word is used in 12.2 for the 'eyes fixed' on Jesus, but the underlying theme in both places is that of endurance in faith.

11.27   The same theme is developed in the next incident in Moses' career. The difficulty with this verse is that Ex. 2.14f. clearly states that Moses 'was alarmed', and therefore 'fled from [the king of Egypt's] presence and went and settled in Midian'. Some have tried to solve the problem by making the present verse refer, not to Moses' flight to Midian, but to Moses reassuring his people when they were frightened at the time of the exodus (14.10–14). This is unlikely, because it refers to an event later than that mentioned in the next verse. The writer of Hebrews is so impressed by Moses' general courage and faith that he apparently neglects the text which says that at one point he was afraid.

The word for *was resolute* may itself suggest fixing one's eyes on something, as in v. 26 where a different word is used. *As one who saw the invisible God* is almost a play on words in the Greek: 'as seeing the unseen'. *God* is implied.

11.28   The establishment of the Passover (Ex. 12.1–20) is closely linked with smearing the blood of sacrificed lambs on the lintel and doorposts of each Israelite house. The purpose of this was that when the Lord saw it he would 'pass over that door and not let the destroyer enter to strike' the firstborn of Israel (v. 23), whereas this tenth plague would kill all the Egyptian firstborn (Ex. 11.4). Hebrews goes further than Exodus in saying, not only that the destroyer would not *strike* the Israelite firstborn, but that he would not even *touch* them (compare comment on 12.20). Once again faith is seen as the alignment of human will with the purposes of God for his people; an anticipation of the obedience of Christ (Heb. 10.5–10).

11.29 On first reading this verse seems a mere summary of Ex. 14.21–31. In fact, the author is probably suggesting to his readers a comparison between their situation and that of the Israelites, who, despite all God had done for them already, approached the crossing of the Red Sea with fear (v. 10), and looked back to the apparently greater safety of Egypt (vv. 11f.). Their attitude in fact now contrasts with Moses' courage, but Hebrews' *by faith they crossed* affirms that the Israelites finally 'put their faith in the LORD and in Moses his servant' (v. 31). Their actions, no doubt, spoke their faith more loudly than their words.

11.30 literally begins: 'By faith the walls of Jericho fell . . .', but *were made to fall* correctly suggests a reference to the faith of the invading Israelite army; see Josh. 6.12–21. The writer of Hebrews may have thought of their faith as consisting in their persistent marching round Jericho, or in their obedience to God's instructions. The writer is not concerned with details of this account, such as the important role of priests or the Ark of the Covenant; nor with any symbolism in the number seven.

11.31 is not concerned with the earlier story of Rahab hiding the Israelite spies (Josh. 2.1–22) before the attack on Jericho; instead, he is concerned with her later rescue from the general destruction of the city (6.17, 22–25). The Old Testament account says that God placed everything in Jericho under a ban; that is, ordered it to be destroyed and not taken as booty (v. 18). The writer of Hebrews may have understood this text to be a condemnation of the inhabitants as *unbelievers*; but in fact this is not given as a reason for the destruction of the city. *Gave them a kindly welcome* recalls Josh 2.4, 6. Hebrews does not stress the fact that a non-Israelite played a part in the working out of God's purpose for his people.

In 11.32–38 the tempo of the narrative progressively increases. This is partly because the writer is less interested in Israelite history after the exodus, but more in order to build up to an effective climax to the chapter in vv. 39f. The passage sounds as if it may have been spoken before it was written down, or written down in order to be spoken.

11.32 The rhetorical question, *Need I say more?* adds to the effect. This is the first time the writer refers to himself as *I*.

He is not concerned to mention these (for his purpose) minor characters in the right order, which is (1) Barak, Judg. 4.6–22; (2) Gideon, Judg. 6.11 – 8.33; (3) Jephthah, Judg. 11.1 – 12.7; (4) Samson, Judg. 13.24 – 16.30; (5) Samuel (I Sam. 1.20 – 4.1; chs. 7 – 13, 15f., 19); (6) David (I Sam. 16.13 – 30.31; II Sam.). The writer names them in three pairs, the more important of each pair being mentioned first. The heaping up of names heightens the tension. Of the six Old Testament figures, only David and Samuel are mentioned elsewhere in the New Testament. David was mentioned as a psalmist in Heb. 4.7, as in Rom. 4.6; 11.9; compare Acts 4.25. In the synoptic gospels, especially Matthew, he is most often referred to as an ancestor of Jesus (e.g. Matt. 12.23; Mark 12.35 and parallels; Luke 18.38f.; compare Rev. 5.5; 22.16). John and Hebrews show comparatively little interest in David. Samuel, linked in the present verse with the prophets, is himself called a prophet in II Chron. 35.18; compare Acts 3.24; 13.20. Although a constant theme of Hebrews is the way in which the Old Testament points forward to Christ, prophets are mentioned only in 1.1 and here; quotations from prophets are not identified by their authors.

11.33f.   The writer is not concerned to match the events in this verse with the names in the last verse. Victories over enemy kingdoms are recorded for Barak (Judg. 4.24), Gideon (Judg. 7); Jephthah (Judg. 11), Samson (Judg. 16), and David (I Sam. 8.1). Only here in the New Testament is faith associated with military victories; contrast Jesus' command, 'Love your enemies', Matt. 5.44. Heb. 11.36ff. will give a higher place to martyrs than to conquerors.

Established justice means not only that the judges themselves behaved justly, but that they upheld and administered justice in Israel. David was said to do this in II Sam. 8.15, and similar language is used of Samuel in I Sam. 12.4, 23.

Saw God's promises fulfilled, literally 'received promises' (RSV), means that they received what God had promised for this life; for example, Israel occupied Canaan, and David took possession of Jerusalem (II Sam. 5.7). There is no contradiction with *they did not receive what was promised* in Heb. 11.39, since this refers to the final fulfilment of God's promises to his people.

They shut the mouths of lions refers most clearly to Daniel (Dan. 6.16–23). In the standard Greek translation of v. 18 it is said that God shut the lions' mouths, but Hebrews follows another translation. Similar feats by Samson (Judg. 14.5f.) and David (I Sam. 17.34f.) are also recorded.

11.34 *Quenched the fury of fire* is another reference to the Book of Daniel, in which Shadrach, Meshach and Abednego are delivered from the fiery furnace (Dan. 3, especially v. 27); see also Num. 11.2; I Macc. 2.59.

Escaped death by the sword is literally 'fled the edges of a sword'; that is, a two-edged sword, as figuratively in 4.12. The word for 'fled' does not usually mean 'escape', but here the idea is that they successfully fled and thus escaped. 11.27 already mentioned Moses' escape from violent death (compare Ex. 18.4). Similar stories are told of David (I Sam. 19.10), Elijah (I Kings 19.2f., 10), Elisha (II Kings 6.12–16). We do not know which of these stories, if any, the writer of Hebrews had particularly in mind.

Their weakness was turned to strength, that is, by God. Samson, mentioned in Heb. 11.37, prayed for strength before using violence in the name of the Lord (Judg. 16.28), and so did Judith (Judith 13.7f.).

They grew powerful in war, like the previous clause, suggests the action of God. It is said of David facing Goliath that

> he called to the Lord Most High,
> who gave strength to his right arm
> to strike that mighty warrior down

(Ecclus. (Ben Sira) 47.5; compare what is said of Joshua in 46.1).

They put foreign armies to rout could refer to any of Israel's victories; perhaps Gideon's attack on the Midianite army (Judg. 7.21ff.), or Barak's onslaught on Sisera and his army (Judg. 4.15f.).

11.35 Less destructive examples of faith now follow, and the pace becomes rather less hectic. The two examples in this verse are concerned, like v. 19, with restoration to life; the first with restoration to life in this world, the second with resurrection beyond death. The *women* in the first part of the verse are the widow of Zarephath (I Kings 17.17–25) and the Shunnamite woman (II Kings 4.18–37); their sons were brought back to life by Elijah and Elisha respectively. The widow of Zarephath begins by asking Elijah: 'What made you interfere?' (I Kings 17.18), but then progresses through passive obedience (v. 19) to her confession of faith to Elijah: 'I know . . . that the word of the LORD on your lips is truth' (v. 24). The writer of Hebrews, as in Heb. 11.11,27, 29, is concerned with her final attitude, by implication commending it to those of his readers who have not yet reached that state.

The second part of v. 35 probably refers to martyrs who lived in the heroic times of the Maccabees: Eleazar (II Macc. 6.18–31; IV Macc. 6f.), his seven sons, and their mother, who was the last to be put to death (II Macc. 7; IV Macc. 8 – 18). The mother's faith is not mentioned specifically in IV Macc. 17.2, and is implied in the whole story of their resolute refusal to accept 'release' at the price of eating pork and so abandoning God's people (compare Heb. 11.25). *Resurrection to a better life*, literally, 'a better resurrection', recalls the *better, more lasting possession* of 10.34, the *better country, a heavenly one* of 11.16, and the *city which is to come* of 13.16.

11.36f.   In these verses, too, the writer is probably thinking of those who suffered under Greek persecution at the time of the Maccabees. The references are mostly too brief and general for us to be sure, but as the climax of the chapter approaches, the writer probably draws closer to his own and his readers' times. *Jeers* is a word translated in II Macc. 7.7 as 'indignities'; there it refers to Eleazar's son being made a laughing-stock and then scalped. Eleazar (II Macc. 6.30; IV Macc. 6.3, 6), his eldest son (IV Macc. 9.12), and his seven sons together (II Macc. 7.1) were all flogged. His seventh son was one of those bound in fetters (IV Macc. 12.3), and the sons of the leading Maccabees were put in prison (I Macc. 9.53), like Samson (Judg. 16.25), and, earlier, members of the community to which Hebrews is addressed (Heb. 10.33).

In v. 37 the pace increases once again. *Stoned to death* probably refers to the prophet Zechariah the son of Jehoiada, whom King Joash ordered to be stoned to death (II Chron. 22.20ff.); a typically Israelite punishment.

Sawn in two probably refers to the tradition, found outside the Bible in pre-Christian times, that Isaiah suffered this fate under King Manasseh.[2]

The word translated 'they were tempted' in the REB footnote is similar in Greek to *they were sawn in two*, and was probably added by mistake. It would in any case be a great anti-climax.

They were put to the sword could refer to various groups of Israel's enemies (for example, Ex. 17.13; Deut. 20.13), but more probably refers to the killing of true prophets under Ahab (I Kings 19.10).

They went about clothed in skins of sheep or goats probably refers to the prophet's typical hairy mantle (Zech. 13.4), such as Elijah handed on to Elisha (I Kings 19.13, 19; II Kings 2.8.13f.).

Deprived of material goods (compare Mark 10.21 and parallels),

[2] *Ascension of Isaiah*, perhaps second century BCE, 5.11–14.

'poor' (GNB); Paul uses the same word in I Cor. 1.7 of being deprived of spiritual gifts. *Oppressed* is related to the noun translated 'tormented' in 10.33, and conveys the same idea of hostile pressure. *Ill-treated* is used of the priest Abiathar having shared David's afflictions (I Kings 2.26); the same word is translated *maltreated* in Heb. 13.3.

11.38 *The world was not worthy of them* is a quiet aside, all the more effective for being thrown into this hectic list of sufferings borne by God's people. Yet it is more than that: it reinforces the point that their real home was in heaven – just as Jesus had no place in the earthly priesthood (8.4), and the patriarchs lived as aliens even in the earthly promised land (11.9f.).

Israel's forty years' wandering in the desert after the exodus left a deep mark on their collective memory. The desert remained a place to which one could retreat for safety, as David did when threatened by Saul (I Sam. 23.14; 24.2); Elijah when threatened by Jezebel (I Kings 19.4), Mattathias and his followers in Maccabean times (I Macc. 2.29, 31), and Judas Maccabaeus with his army (I Macc. 5.24, 28; 9.33). Similarly the hills were a place of refuge, for Israel from the Midianites (Judg. 6.2); for Elijah on Mount Horeb (I Kings 19.8), and for Mattathias and his sons (I Macc. 2.28). Among those who are said to have taken refuge in caves are Israel when attacked by the Philistines (I Sam 13.6), David in the cave of Adullam (I Sam. 22.1), a hundred prophets hidden by Obadiah (I Kings 18.4); Elijah (I Kings 19.9), Jews threatened by Ptolemy (II Macc. 6.11), and Judas Maccabaeus and his companions (II Macc. 10.6). Moses (Ex. 33.22) and Samson (Judg. 15.11) are said to have hidden in 'holes in the ground', like caves but smaller.

11.39 God testifies in Scripture his approval of these heroes of faith; his promises to them will not be broken. But on any but the earthly level they have not yet received what God promised. Verse 40 will say why. The present verse is a summary, similar to the first part of v. 13. There is no contradiction with 3.16–19, where the writer is thinking of the people as a whole, not of individuals, and where he is warning, not as here encouraging. The writer will state more fully in the next chapter (vv. 12ff., 21–24) what it is that God promised in the past, and is now ready to give to all his people together.

As elsewhere (vv. 2, 4), references to God's *approval* are to the testimony of Scripture.

11.40 In the early chapters an essential result of Christ's exaltation to God's right hand was seen as his *bringing many sons to glory* (2.10). The *Son* and the *sons* (or *children*, 2.13) are not to be separated. The central chapters spoke of Jesus as the *forerunner* (6.20) of those who believe, and as the one through whom the readers may now approach God (8.1; 10.19). The writer now draws the Old Testament heroes into this picture of God's purpose. They are not merely examples, like the bad example of Israel cited in 3.7 – 4.11. Just as the bad example of Israel was an opportunity for the present generation (4.9), so here the good examples from Israel's past are explained as a reason for them to be at last caught up into the fulfilment of God's plan for his whole people. Until now Israel's history has been one of frustrated hopes on the one hand and persistent faith on the other. Now, and only now through Christ, their hopes can be fulfilled and their faith rewarded. But all this hinges on the believing response of the present generation, that is, the readers of Hebrews; for they have, as earlier generations did not, Jesus as their high priest (8.1; 9.11). REB seems to understand the *better plan* (similarly GNB; literally, 'something better', RSV, NIV, NJB) as the fact *that only with us should they reach perfection*. This is possible; but in any case the writer will say more, especially in 12.21–24, about this 'something better', in which all generations of God's people are about to share.

12.1–13   *Faith today*

12.1f. form a single sentence in Greek. Verse 1 speaks mainly of 'us'; v. 2 mainly of Jesus. Neither has been much mentioned in ch. 11. An emphatic *therefore*, the first word of the Greek sentence, nevertheless links ch. 12 closely to what has gone before. As 11.40 has just suggested, the readers are the latest in the generations of faith. On their faithfulness to Christ, their high priest, the whole of God's purpose for his people depends.

In v. 1 the writer places himself alongside his readers as *we*, and he will return emphatically to *we* in v. 25. Most of the passage in between will be 'you' language, used both in warning (vv. 4–17) and in encouragement (vv. 18–24).

The *great cloud of witnesses* is thought of, not as witnesses to what God has done for them, but as spectators watching to see how the readers run their race of faith. The Greek word for 'witness', *martus*, is related to the English word 'martyr', since martyrs were defined as those who had died as witnesses to their faith. The word does not yet have this special meaning here, though it may have in Revelation (for example, 17.6).

Translations appear to distinguish between *every emcumbrance* and *the sin that . . . restricts us*. The second expression may be more specific than the first, or the meaning may be: 'every encumbrance, that is, the sin that . . . restricts us.' In both expressions, the picture is one of an athlete stripping himself for a race.

All too readily restricts is literally 'easily surrounding'; 'sin that clings so closely' NRSV, similarly NJB: 'the sin which holds on to us so tightly', GNB; 'the sin that so easily entangles', NIV. Two good manuscripts have a similar word which probably means 'easily distracting'.

Resolution takes up again the theme of holding on to faith. The same word was translated *endurance* in 10.36, and the related verb in 10.32 was translated *held firm*. The verb is used to Jesus as one who *endured* the cross (12.2) and *submitted to* opposition (v. 3), and again of the readers enduring God's fatherly discipline (v. 7).

12.2 The order of words in the first part of the verse emphasizes *Jesus*, as in 2.9: literally, 'looking steadily to the pioneer and perfecter of our faith Jesus'. 'Looking steadily' may be intended as an instruction, as in GNB: 'Let us keep our eyes fixed on Jesus.' *Pioneer* recalls the same word in 2.20, and *perfecter* recalls *make . . . perfect*, also in 2.10. Jesus is the one 'on whom our faith depends from beginning to end' (GNB).

For the sake of the joy that lay ahead of him is the most likely meaning of the following words. Another possibility is: 'Instead of (earthly) joy which lay within his grasp, he endured the cross and thus obtained greater joy in heaven'; the meaning would be similar to what was said of Moses in 11.25, though without the reference to sin. More likely is the interpretation which underlies REB and other translations. This is that Jesus saw the end of his mission from the beginning, perhaps even from before he became man. This disgrace of the cross thus became, like the incarnation in 2.9, something to be endured *for a little while*, because of the joy and glory which would follow. (The theme of disgrace was touched on in different words in 10.33.) In the same way, God's discipline of his children is only *for a short time . . . so that we may share his holiness* (12.10).

Ignoring its disgrace, literally 'despising the shame' (RSV) is a tightly packed paradox: Jesus himself despised the shame by which he was himself despised (compare Isa. 53.3).

The end of the verse is familiar traditional teaching, based on Ps. 110.1; compare Heb. 1.3,13.

12.3 develops a little further the thought of what Jesus suffered, and begins to apply it to the readers' situation. The rather unusual word translated *think* (also in GNB, NJB; 'consider', RSV, NIV) is used in II Macc. 12.43 of an action by which Judas Maccabaeus 'took due account of the resurrection'.

Submitted to such opposition from sinners is literally 'endured from sinners such opposition against himself' (compare RSV). The words 'against himself' sound as if they go without saying, which is no doubt why REB omits them. Some excellent manuscripts, however, have the puzzling wording 'against themselves'. This may be an echo of Num. 16.38, where Korah and others, who set up an unauthorized form of worship, are said to have done so 'at the cost of their lives.' If so, the present verse may mean that Jesus' enemies did harm to themselves, bringing about their own destruction. On the basis of this text, the words are a warning to the readers.

The word translated *grow faint* is the same as that translated *be discouraged* in Heb. 12.5; the idea is that of weariness, as in Mark. 8.3 and parallel; Gal. 6.9.

12.4 *Struggle* may suggest, like vv. 1f., an athletic competition. Similar language is used in connection with Judas Maccabaeus who 'exhorted his troops to fight nobly to the death' (II Macc. 13.14). *Sin* in this context is not primarily inward temptation but outward opposition, such as Jesus himself endured (v. 3). *Shedding your blood* is literally 'blood'; REB makes it clear that what is meant is the death of a martyr; 'you have not yet had to resist to the point of being killed', GNB. There is no suggestion here, at least directly, of blood shed in sacrifice, as frequently in ch. 9.

12.5f. *You have forgotten* (also NIV) may also be translated 'have you forgotten . . . ?' (RSV, GNB, NJB); this is rather less natural, since v. 4 was a statement. *As sons* picks out in advance the key word of the quotation from Prov. 3.11f. The readers really are sons (and daughters) of God (2.10), though some of them are in danger of losing that status (6.9). The original setting in Proverbs is that of a sage addressing one of his pupils; but no particular individual is mentioned there, so the saying is open to be reapplied to others, as here in Hebrews.

The word for *discipline*, used also in Eph. 6.4 and II Tim. 3.16, has a range of meaning which runs from training and education to corporal punishment. The writer of Hebrews quotes the words *he chastises*, which literally means 'he beats with a whip', but does not comment on them. In the Greek of Deut. 12.2, the exodus is described as God's discipline of his people, as is Israel's suffering under persecution in II Macc. 6.12–17 and *Psalms of Solomon* 8. More generally, discipline through suffering is a constant theme in the Book of Judges (for example, 3.7ff.,12–15; 4.1ff.).

The point of the quotation is that, just as discipline is an essential element in the relationship between human fathers and their sons, so it is in the relationship in which God *acknowledges* any human being as his son. The language focuses on male children, as on God as father, but there is no suggestion that daughters are excluded, or that God is thought of as distinctively male. It will soon become clear that the writer is thinking particularly of God 'acknowledging' believers in the final judgment (compare Matt. 10.32 and parallel). Endurance of God's discipline is another aspect of persistence in faith; even persecution (vv. 3f.) is seen as ultimately being used by God.

12.7f.   The last part of v. 7 is a rhetorical question meaning: 'Every father disciplines his sons.' Logically, therefore, in the case of a father who does not discipline his son, one side of the relationship must not be genuine. Since it is unthinkable that God should not be a true father, it therefore follows that the son in question is not a true son; that is, that he is illegitimate. The argument cannot be pressed any further, but its point is to alert the readers to the danger of losing their membership of God's people if they do not bear the discipline of persecution patiently. The word for *share* is the same as that translated *partners* in 3.1,14.

The best commentary on this passage is Wisdom 3, which combines the themes of discipline, legitimate and illegitimate parents, rebellion against God, and the final judgment.

12.9   More encouragingly, the writer introduces one of his 'how much more' arguments (see comment on 2.2f.). The rhetorical question in the second part of the verse is equivalent to a strong positive statement: 'we should submit even more readily . . .'. REB brings out the meaning well, but RSV preserves the balance between the two halves of the verse: '. . . We have had earthly fathers to discipline us and we respected them. Shall we not much more be subject to the

Father of spirits and live?' The future tense 'shall live' suggests eternal life.

12.10   like v. 9, is divided into two contrasting halves, the first about human fathers and the second about God as Father. The point of the contrast is not that a human father disciplines his son only *for a short time* (literally, 'for a few days'), whereas God's discipline goes on for ever; the writer's present purpose is encouragement, not warning as in v. 8. Both periods of discipline are limited. The difference between them is that human discipline is limited by fallible judgment and can make mistakes, whereas God's discipline of his children has as its purpose *our true welfare* (literally, 'for the general good', NJB); more specifically, *so that we may share his holiness*. The contrast between temporal pain and eternal happiness has a long history:

> O happy band of pilgrims,
>   Look upward to the skies,
> Where such a light affliction,
>   Shall win you such a prize.[1]

The reward of believers is not only to form a people set apart for God, but to share together the life of God himself.

12.11   summarizes what has been said about discipline. On the one hand (*to be sure* is implied), it is temporarily unpleasant. We, unlike Jesus (v. 2), cannot see the joy beyond the pain. But on the other hand, the results of discipline, for those who successfully complete the training, are peace and righteousness. The one grows from the other as fruit and crops grow from seed.

It is remarkable that vv. 4–11 contain no direct reference to Christ, but deal entirely with believers' relationship with God as Father. This passage in fact stands in the Old Testament wisdom tradition, for example in the books of Proverbs and Wisdom. There is no radical reinterpretation of the quotation from Prov. 3.11f., as there is of quotations in ch. 1 and elsewhere which are applied to Christ.

12.12f.   The writer smoothly turns his attention to relations between stronger and weaker Christians. He has touched on this theme in passing in 10.32f., and it will be more important in 12.14–17 and in ch. 13.

---

[1] John Mason Neale, after Joseph the Hymnographer (9th century); 'O happy band of pilgrims', *MHB* 618, v. 7.

These verses use illustrations from medical practice at the time, mediated through Scripture. Verse 12 echoes Isa. 35.3:

> Brace the arms that are limp,
> steady the knees that give way;

part of a generally hopeful passage; compare Ecclus. (Ben Sira) 25.23. Verse 13 echoes Prov. 4.26:

> Mark out the path that your feet must take,
> and your ways will be secure.

In the Greek of the following verse, it is said that the Lord 'will make your paths straight'. This passage is close to the one quoted in Heb. 12.5f. The point of the quotation in Hebrews is that spiritually ailing members of the community must either progress to full health, or fall into a state worse than that from which they began their Christian life. The present verses are thus a more concise and milder form of the warning in 6.4ff.

12.14–29   *Life under the new order*

Titles given to the section vary: 'Warning against Rejecting God's Grace' (United Bible Societies' Greek New Testament, similarly NIV); 'Instructions and Warnings' (GNB); the REB title *The fruit of righteousness* also covers ch. 13. The main reason for this variety is not that the section is confused. On the contrary, it consists of three distinct paragraphs, the first (vv. 14–17) containing warnings for the readers; the second (vv. 18–24) contrasting life under the old and the new orders; and the third (vv. 25–29) pointing to the final 'shaking' of the universe. But within this general pattern warning and encouragement are so closely combined that it is difficult to separate them. In the first paragraph warning predominates, yet even here, the writer sets before his readers the hope of 'seeing the Lord' (v. 14). The second paragraph contains more encouragement than warning, yet even in the positive part, the central figure is *God the judge of all* (v. 23). The third paragraph speaks of the final cataclysm, and its final word is about God as *a devouring fire*; yet the central message is the encouraging one that *the kingdom we are given is unshakeable* (v. 28). A key question will concern the central paragraph: is *the heavenly Jerusalem* (vv. 22ff.) intended to sound more or less fearsome than

Mount Sinai (vv. 18–21)? Or is the point of contrast between the two something different?

12.14   The theme of peace is taken up from *peaceful* in v. 11. The writer's main concern in these closing chapters is with relations within the Christian community, but there is no reason to doubt that *everyone* means what it says. The writer does not, however, say that it will always be possible to maintain peaceful relations with non-Christians. As Paul put it, 'If possible, so far as it lies with you, live at peace with all' (Rom. 12.18).

Holiness in v. 10 meant the holiness of God himself; here a different but related word is used for the process or event by which his people become holy: 'Try to live a holy life' (GNB); 'Make every effort . . . to be holy' (NIV). There is no contradiction (though, as we know today, there may be tension) between peaceful relations with those outside the Christian community, and living the life of God's special people.

The Lord, as usual in Hebrews (but not in Paul), means God the Father, not Christ. There is no separation between daily Christian living and expectation of the last days.

12.15f.   The word translated *take heed* (NJB 'be careful'; NIV 'see to it') suggests watchful care. The word is related to the term for a bishop, but the writer does not assign the task of caring to any individuals within the community. Conversely (v. 15), if any individual goes astray, the whole community is put in danger.

Three dangers are mentioned: alternatively, the same danger is described from three points of view in progressively stronger and more detailed terms.

(1) The word for *forfeit* is the one used in Rom. 3.23 of sinners being 'deprived' of God's glory (so NJB here). The basic meaning of the word is 'lack', but even allowing for the writer's approaching a painful subject gently, something stronger seems intended here. NRSV's 'fails to obtain' reflects the theme of the whole epistle; NIV 'misses'. Any failure to obtain God's grace must come from human sin, not from any limitation on God's love. Hebrews speaks with equal naturalness about *reward* (10.35) and *grace:* God's reward for human faithfulness is itself a gift.

(2) The second warning recalls Deut. 29.17 in Greek. The standard Greek text has 'lest there be in you a root springing up with gall and bitterness'; the writer in Hebrews probably followed a slightly different text. The metaphor of the *root* suggests something which is

in danger of growing and multiplying. *Bitter* probably suggests contamination, going bad, rather than disappointment, as often in English. The Greek word is related to the word for *rebellion* used in Heb. 3.8 = Ps. 95.8. The word translated *noxious* in the present verse means generally 'to cause trouble' (so GNB, NIV, NJB); it is used in Luke 6.18 of those 'troubled with unclean spirits'. The word translated *contaminate* suggests a defilement which, unless checked, will destroy the holiness (v. 14) of God's people.

(3) (v. 16). The third warning extends the second, and is itself extended into v. 17. *Immoral* literally refers to sexual immorality, as in 13.4 and in I Cor. 5.9f. In the present verse it is the purity of the believing community which is at stake, so there are probably also overtones of unfaithfulness to God, as often in the Old Testament.

Similarly, *worldly-minded*, 'unspiritual' (GNB), or 'godless' (NIV) means profane as opposed to holy; thinking and behaving like an unbeliever, not like a member of God's special people. This attitude is illustrated by the example of Esau (Gen. 25.33f.), who put a lower value on his rights as the elder son than on the immediate satisfaction of physical hunger. Later Jewish tradition suggested that Esau's foreign wives (Gen. 26.34; 36.2f.) led him into heathen practices. The writer of Hebrews, however, stays close to the biblical account.

12.17   The end of Esau's story (Gen. 27.30–40) is close to what the writer fears for some of his readers. Esau came to regret having virtually given away his rights as the elder son, and *wanted to claim the blessing*. This goes a little further than the Old Testament story, in which Esau merely says to Jacob: 'Father, bless me too' (Gen. 27.34). In the present text, *the blessing* means the blessing which should have belonged to the elder son. *Claim* is the word translated 'inherit' in Heb. 1.4, meaning 'receive as a gift', in this case from Isaac. The writer fears that some of his readers may fail to obtain the blessing which God has in store for his people (11.39f.) and which he will shortly describe (12.22ff.). In other words, he fears that God will in the end 'reject' them, as Isaac in effect rejected Esau.

REB makes it clear that *begged for it* means 'begged for the blessing', rather than 'begged for a way to change what he had done' (GNB text). *Change of mind* is the word commonly translated 'repentance'. *Change of mind* is appropriate for Esau; but the danger for the readers is that of putting themselves in a position in which *it is impossible to bring them afresh to repentance* (6.6). Gen. 27.38 states that 'Esau wept bitterly'.

12.18–24 may be called the rhetorical climax of Hebrews. In two impressive sentences (vv. 18–21,22ff.), the writer builds up contrasting pictures of the giving of the old covenant, and of life under the new covenant. The central feature of the first picture is its fearsomeness. The second picture is fearsome too, since it includes *God the judge of all* (v. 23), and the writer will follow it with another warning (v. 25); but it is dominated by what Jesus had done, and by the effects of his sacrifice.

It is noticeable that the first picture is largely filled by impersonal forces, while *the people* by contrast play a rather passive role. One of the Old Testament accounts specifies that Israel 'saw no form of any kind' (Deut. 4.15, compare v. 12); they only heard God's voice. The second picture, by contrast, is crowded with human and supernatural beings; the whole family of God, now at last (see 11.39f.) gathered together in the heavenly *city* (see 11.16) which previous generations sought so long in vain on earth. This is the 'something better' mentioned in 11.40, which the writer is afraid that some of his readers might 'forfeit' (12.15).

The contrast between the two pictures is made clear by repetition of a weighty Greek word translated *you have come*. This verb in Hebrews suggests approaching or entering God's presence in worship (see comment on 4.16). There is no necessary suggestion of *only* drawing near, but not actually gaining access to God, so *come* is a widely accepted translation. Certain details in vv. 22ff., however, suggest that the readers' hopes, however keen, have not yet been fully realized (13.14). God has not yet held his final judgment, so the writer knows that his readers are not yet fully integrated in the assembly of those whose *spirits* have been *made perfect* (v. 23). The form of the verb suggests a lasting condition. The implications of this will be drawn out in vv. 26ff., especially in the *unshakeable kingdom* of v. 28.

The blazing fire of Sinai is literally 'what may be touched, a blazing fire' (RSV), but the reference is clearly to Sinai, and REB makes this clear; many manuscripts have 'a mountain that may be touched'. The writer draws together details from various parts of the Pentateuch, including Ex. 19.16–22; 20.18–21; Deut. 4.11f.; 5.22–27; 9.19. The form of the word for *blazing* is different from that used in Deut. 4.11, and may suggest that the fire has been supernaturally kindled. Deuteronomy says that 'the mountain . . . was ablaze with fire to the very skies'. Deuteronomy in fact refers to a manifestation of God on Mount Horeb, but this is merged in Hebrews with the Exodus account of the giving of the law on Mount Sinai. Ex. 20.18f. tells how, when the people saw the lightning, and the mountain in smoke, and heard the thunder and the trumpet, 'they were afraid and trembled. . . . and said to Moses, "Speak to us yourself and we will listen; but do not let God speak to us or we shall die." '

12.20 is a condensed and heightened version of Ex. 19.12f. The added emphasis in Hebrews can be seen in the underlined words of the literal translation: 'If even a wild animal touches the mountain, however lightly, it will be stoned.'

12.21 In Deut. 9 Moses tells how he came down from Mount Horeb with the two stone tablets on which the law had been written; saw the people worshipping the cast image of a bull-calf; flung the tablets down on the ground so that they shattered; and went for forty days without food or drink, because he 'was in dread of the LORD's anger' (v. 19). This is the basis of the present verse; the writer of Hebrews does not seem interested in the precise Old Testament context, which is later than the giving of the law itself. *Appalling* is the word translated *terrifying* in Heb. 10.27,31.

12.22 The second picture is strongly contrasted with the first: *No. . . ,* 'on the contrary'.

The writer does not say exactly how the readers *have come to the heavenly Jerusalem;* no doubt in their life as a Christian community and especially in their worship. Worship is a central theme of Hebrews, yet the author gives little information about the forms of worship used by the people to whom he writes. It is not even certain that they celebrated the Lord's Supper, but see the comment on 13.15. From Paul's descriptions of Christian meetings at Corinth it is clear that they embraced a wider range of activities than what a modern congregation would call 'worship'; for example, it could include disciplinary trials (I Cor. 5.3ff.), though these are not mentioned in Hebrews. One writer, speaking of the Qumran community, has said that 'the whole of the community's life, as well as the whole of the community's history, was considered an all-inclusive liturgy'.[1] A similar spirit breathes through the present passage.

The first three expressions, *Mount Zion, the city of the living God, the heavenly Jerusalem* refers to the same thing, not to the earthly Mount Zion on which the Temple was built.

[1] D. Patte, *Early Jewish Hermeneutics in Palestine* (Studies in Biblical Literature Dissertation Series 22), Richmond, Va. 1975, p. 292.

The writer now passes from the city itself to its inhabitants. The construction of the next few words, and even the exact point at which v. 23 begins, are uncertain. The two main options are: (1) 'to innumerable angels in festal gathering, [23] and to the assembly of the first-born . . .' (RSV text, similarly NIV, NJB), and (2) 'to innumerable angels, [23] and to the festal gathering and assembly of the first-born . . .' (RSV note, similarly GNB, REB). The first option makes a more balanced sentence. The writer, however, is not concerned at this point with precise description, but with the heaping up of impressive details, so the difference is not very important.

Myriads, literally tens of thousands, so 'innumerable' (RSV), 'thousands upon thousands' (NIV). *Festal gathering* may echo Isa. 66.10 in Greek, which uses a related verb meaning 'exult'. *Assembly* is the word elsewhere translated 'church', but here as in the Old Testament (especially Ps. 22.22, quoted in Heb. 2.12) it has a more general meaning.

The firstborn who are enrolled in heaven should not be taken literally. Firstborn sons were considered to belong specially to God (Ex. 13.13; 34.20; compare Num. 18.15), just as God's chosen people were descended from Jacob, who had the status of the elder son (Heb. 11.20). There was a widespread belief that God kept a book in which people's names, or deeds, or both, were recorded (see Ex. 32.32f.; Ps. 139.16; Isa. 4.3; Luke 10.40; Rev. 3.5).

God the judge of all is the construction chosen by most translations, but the words may be more literally translated 'a judge who is God of all' (RSV). The writer does not suggest that the final judgment has yet taken place.

The spirits of good men made perfect is more literally 'the spirits of righteous who have been made perfect'. Such language must refer to human beings rather than angels, but does not exclude women. *Made perfect*, here as usual in Hebrews, means that they have completed their course and safely reached the end of their journey; the verb suggests a permanent state. The readers are eagerly expecting to join them, but have not yet done so, since some can still fall away.

12.24 More prominent in this passage even than God is Jesus, who is again described as the one who 'arranged' a 'new covenant' (GNB). A different word for *new* was used in 8.6; 9.15, but there is no difference in meaning here. Here as in 8.6; 9.15, the new covenant is said to have been sealed with Christ's blood (see also I Peter 1.2). The writer is probably thinking of the blood 'flung' over the people at the inauguration of the Sinai covenant (Ex. 24.8, quoted in Heb. 9.20), though the wording is different.

The apparently abrupt mention of Abel points back to 11.4. It is usually understood to mean that just as the blood of Abel is still, so to speak, crying out (Gen. 4.10) for vengeance against Cain, so the blood of Jesus is still crying out for mercy on sinners who need his sacrifice in order to gain access to God. There may, however, be more comparison than contrast, if, as is possible, the reference is not to Abel's own blood, but to the blood of his sacrifice, the first acceptable sacrifice mentioned in the Bible (Gen. 4.4). The words *the blood of*, before Abel, are not in the text, but are generally understood to be implied.

By now we recognize *better* as one of the writer's favourite words (see comment on 1.4), and one typical of his 'how much more' style of argument.

In the end, the contrast between the old covenant and the new is not primarily that between terror and joy (though that is a consequence for those who hold on to their faith); it is that between a lesser and a greater message from God (see again 1.1–4). The readers have had the greater revelation set out as attractively as possible before them; now they know that have no hope if they ignore or reject it.

The mainly warning passage *12.25–29* immediately follows.

12.25   It is not certain whether 'the voice that speaks' is that of Jesus, as in v. 24, or God, as in vv. 28f. and in 1.1–4. It is not impossible that the writer thinks of Jesus, before his incarnation, as shaking the earth in Old Testament times (v. 26), and as addressing his people now from the 'place' to which he has ascended in heaven. It is not even impossible that he deliberately leaves the matter vague, or makes a gradual transition from Jesus to God. Most commentators, however, choose the simpler option that the whole of vv. 25–29 is about God.

The rest of the verse is a clear 'how much more' argument, closely similar to 2.2f., and less closely to 10.28f. The contrast is between *those who refused* to listen to God (or Christ) speaking to Israel at the time of the exodus, and *we* whom he now addresses from heaven; both the pronouns are emphatic. The first group may be those who heard and begged to *hear no more* (v. 19). Alternatively, the writer may by now be thinking more generally of those who disobeyed God in Old Testament times, thereby making the new covenant necessary (8.7).

12.26   The writer goes over the contrast a second time for good

measure, giving Old Testament evidence for the second ('new covenant') part as well as the first. In the Old Testament it is often said that
the earth, mountains, or sea are shaken (for example, Ex. 19.18; Ps.
18.7.; Judg. 5.4f.; Ps. 68.8; 98.7; compare Judith 5.4f.). It is implied
that the shaking is done by God, and Hebrews says so directly.
Similarly in the New Testament, for example Mark 13.25 and parallels;
Acts 4.31; 16.26; Rev. 6.13, often in passages which speak of the end.

Then and *now* are strongly contrasted. What God has *now* . . .
promised (Hag. 2.6) sounds in fact more like a threat; but as the writer
of Hebrews will show, the shaking of the old universe is only
preliminary to the revelation of an eternal universe which can never
be shaken.

Hebrews quotes Haggai from the Greek Old Testament, adding
not only and *but . . . also* to make the point clear. *The earth* and *the
heavens* means the old universe as a whole, so Hebrews omits Haggai's
further references to the shaking of the sea and the dry land. *The
heavens* here probably means the higher part of the old universe (=
'sky') rather than, as in 1.10 and elsewhere, the immediate presence
of God.

12.27   The writer's concern for his readers leads him to give to the
quotation from Haggai a different meaning from that which the
words had in their Old Testament context. Haggai speaks of the
'shaking' of foreign nations, followed by the setting up in Jerusalem
of a restored temple, richer than the one which existed there before
the exile. The writer of Hebrews has already shown that the old
system of worship has no future in God's purpose (8.13; 10.9). The
word translated *removal* may also mean 'transformation', but *removal*
probably suits the context better here. The upper and lower parts of
the visible universe will be removed. The writer does not say outright
that they will be totally destroyed, but this may be implied. He calls
the old universe *created*, implying that the universe which survives
the 'shaking' shares in some way in the eternal nature of God. This
in turn implies that the unshakeable universe has been in existence
all the time, but will not been clearly seen until after the final
upheaval. It is not clear whether the eternal universe is thought of as
surviving the 'shaking', or as escaping it altogether.

12.28   *The kingdom we are given* is no doubt the same as the *city with
firm foundations* mentioned in 11.10, the *country of their own* of 11.14,
and the *eternal inheritance* of 9.15 (compare 11.8). 'Which we are given'
is literally 'which we are receiving', that is, from God. The writer stops

short of saying that Christians have already received it. Christians do however already have the access to God which is the essence of true worship.

Christians must not neglect to use this access. (The writer now includes himself, returning to the 'we' language of vv. 1f.) In particular, they must do so *with reverence and awe*. That is, they must let God be God in their lives; not, like Esau (vv. 16f.), giving a higher place to worldly values.

12.29 The warning concludes with a virtual quotation of Deut. 4.24, where Moses reminds Israel: 'the LORD your God is a devouring fire, a jealous God' (compare Heb. 10.27). The Bible, unlike some other religious traditions, does not strictly identify God with fire; but fire is a sign of his presence and activity, especially in judgment (compare 1.7; 10.31).

13.1–19   *How to please God*

This last chapter discusses a number of matters not closely connected with one another, but all related to the common life of the Christian community, which has been the theme and purpose of Hebrews as a whole. The style and content are thus rather different, as one might expect, from the great doctrinal passages of Hebrews; but not so different as to prove that ch. 13 is by a different author, as some have thought. In particular, the writer's concern for worship appears here as strongly as anywhere else: only now, it is more for the regular worship of the community to which he writes (compare 10.25), and less for the sacrificial death of Christ (but see 13.12f.,20).

13.1 RSV's literal translation is: 'Let brotherly love continue.' In the ancient world it was unusual for people to speak of one another as brothers unless they were physically related in some way, though not necessarily as sons of the same parents (see comment on 3.1). So 'brotherly love' (Greek *philadelphia*) does not mean merely love like that which brothers have for one another. It means the love of those who really do consider one another as brothers and sisters – though in the case of Christians, not as physically related. This is the basis for the translation: *Never cease to love your fellow-Christians*. NRSV's 'let mutual love continue' is too general. REB translates the same word, 'love of the Christian community' in Rom. 12.10; 'love of the brotherhood' in II Thess. 4.9; and 'brotherly affection' in II Peter 1.7; compare I Peter 1.22. Such love is an essential part of a right relationship with God (Heb. 12.28). The writer reminds the readers of the need to go on loving one another, but he does not see any reason to say why: it is an elementary condition for Christians living together. Nor does the writer discuss the matter at length; there do not seem to be the divisions in his church which Paul encountered at Corinth (I Cor. 1, though see Heb. 13.9).

13.2 In Rom. 12.9f., Paul mentions first 'love' (by implication, for everyone), then 'love of the Christian community'. Hebrews is more concerned for relationships between Christians, though he commended *peace with everyone* in 12.14. *Hospitality* is probably directed mainly if not entirely towards fellow-Christians. It was particularly important in a far-flung but closely-knit community such as the early church, where evangelists and others were constantly on the move. See Mark 1.29ff.; 2.15ff.; 14.3ff; and parallels; Luke 10.3f.; 14.12ff.; Rom. 12.13f.; I Tim. 3.2; Titus 1.8; I Peter 4.9.

Neglect to show is literally 'forget' (see also v. 16); Paul was similarly asked by the leaders of the church in Jerusalem to 'keep in mind the poor' (Gal. 2.10).

The second part of the verse gives a motive for hospitality. Abraham and Sarah welcomed 'three men' (Gen. 18.2–26), one of whom promised that she would have a son. These visitors are apparently identified with the 'two angels' (Gen. 19.1; compare vv. 15f.) who visited Lot in Sodom, but declined his offer of hospitality (v. 2).

13.3 This verse contains two more practical appeals, each with a motive. The writer has already mentioned imprisonment in 10.34. This was clearly a persistent danger for his readers (compare 13.23), as was more general ill-treatment (see 10.33). Christians must identify with one another as much as possible, especially when some are bearing the stigma (v. 13) of imprisonment. *Vulnerable* is an imaginative but correct translation of 'in the body' (rsv); they are still in this life, exposed to mortal ills. Calvin thought that 'in the body' meant 'in the church', as sometimes in Paul; but this is unlikely here.

13.4 If Christians are unfaithful to their marriage partners, the whole Christian community will be harmed, since its corporate life depends on openness and faithfulness. The writer thinks of this harm as the spiritual counterpart of ritual defilement; it made people unfit for worship. *The marriage bond* must *be kept inviolate* overlaps in meaning with *marriage must be honoured by all*, but is more specific. At this point Christian and Old Testament ethics reinforce one another; compare particularly Wisd. 3.13. *God will judge* recalls Heb. 10.30, which quotes Deut. 32.36. Fornication is sexual immorality in general, as distinct from adultery which involves a married person. The words for *fornicators and adulterers* are grammatically masculine, but include women as well as men.

13.5f.   *Do not live for money* is an idiomatic translation of what is literally: 'un-moneyloving the way (of life)'. *Be content with what you have* says practically the same thing in a positive form. This instruction is no more specifically Christian than that in v. 4; in the same spirit, John the Baptist told soldiers to make do with their pay (Luke 3.14).

There follow two Old Testament quotations, not reinterpreted in a Christian sense, which support the appeal to trust God rather than money (compare Matt. 6.24–34 and parallel). The first question (v. 5) is probably from Deut. 31.6, but similar language is found in Deut. 31.8; Gen. 28.15; Josh. 1.5, and I Chron. 28.20).

The second quotation (v. 6) is taken from Ps. 118.6, a psalm much used in the New Testament, which speaks of persecution (v. 5), faith (v. 8), hope (v. 9), and discipline (v. 18), all themes found in Hebrews. *The Lord* is God.

13.7   Verses 7 and 17 mention *your leaders*; almost certainly past leaders in v. 7, and present leaders in v. 17. Most of the passage in between is concerned with worship, which may suggest that conducting worship was one of the leaders' duties. The writer, perhaps out of modesty, does not claim to be one of the leaders himself (contrast Paul, for example I Cor. 4.14f.); he is certainly not an apostle (see comment on 2.3). There is however a natural transition from the leaders in v. 17 to the writer in vv. 18f.

Another of the leaders' duties was to speak God's message, that is, to give Christian preaching and teaching; perhaps at first to bring the news about Jesus (see 2.3). They are held up as an example to the readers precisely because they held on to their faith to the end (see 3.6,14). Since they have died, they are now beyond the danger of apostasy. There is no evidence that these leaders died as martyrs; indeed 12.4 suggests the opposite. Both their lives and the manner of their death are held up as examples: 'Think back on how they lived and died' (GNB). The supreme example of Christ (I Peter 2.21) does not make lesser examples unnecessary (compare I Cor. 4,16; Phil. 3.17; I Thess. 1.7; II Thess. 3.9).

13.8   The author rises rather suddenly from practical instructions and recommendations, in order to 'fix his eyes' (compare 12.2) once more on Jesus, who will be central to vv. 9–15.20f. The verse sums up, in language similar to that used of God in Rev. 1.4, what has been said earlier about Christ's eternal being (1.3,8,10), his present ministry in heaven (8.1; 10.21f.; 12.24), and his future role (1.2,12; 9.28). Through it all he remains the same (compare 1.12), utterly faithful to God's unchanging purpose, and thus the greatest example of faithfulness for the readers (see v. 7).

13.9   This and the next few verses, like some other parts of the New Testament, would be easier to understand if we knew more about the situation of the writer of Hebrews and his first readers. This much, however, is clear: Jesus Christ, always the same (v. 8) is contrasted with a multiplicity of teachings alien to the gospel, and these teachings have something to do with food. Now food created problems for the early Christians' dealings with pagans, as can be seen from Rom. 14 and I Cor. 8. Most of the first readers of Hebrews, however, were probably Jews; the writer has already contrasted Christ's priesthood and sacrifice with Jewish *external ordinances . . . concerned with food and drink* (9.10). This is probably the main contrast he has in mind here too, though *all sorts* may include pagan teachings and practices also. Such teachings, and the practices they involve, whether Jewish or pagan, would 'sweep' Christians off their *course;* similar language to *drifting from our course* in 2.1, but stronger. Such teachings do not lead one to rely on God's grace ('God's' is implied), or give inner strength (literally, 'strengthen the heart', which means much the same as 'give the worshipper a clear conscience and so bring him to perfection' in 9.9). They 'have not benefited' (RSV; REB's 'never' is implied) *those who observed them.* 'Did not benefit' uses the same verb as *did them no good* in 4.2. In a similar setting Jesus says: 'It is the spirit that gives life; the flesh can achieve nothing' (John 6.63). The writer of Hebrews is always concerned, not with ritual as an end in itself, but with the good which worship does; of course the good in question is the highest, spiritual good.

13.10   The word translated *sacred tent* is the same as that translated *altar* in 7.13; the two verses complement one another. Just as Jesus had no place in the levitical priesthood, so God does not authorize Jewish priests to share in Christian sacred meals.

This way of putting it is a slight anachronism: the writer of Hebrews does not speak, as we do, of 'Jewish' and 'Christian'; and in v. 12 he will speak without distinction of the people of God. Whereas Paul, as apostle to the Gentiles, has to proclaim loudly that the barriers between Jews and Gentiles have been broken down in Christ (I Cor. 1.24; 12.13), the author of Hebrews, writing mainly to Jews, keeps the door open for all his readers to retain their place as members of God's people.

The present verse, like v. 11, probably refers to the liturgy of the annual Day of Atonement, described in Lev. 16; there were references to this chapter in Heb. 9, especially vv. 7 and 13. Part of this liturgy involved the sacrifice of a bull and a goat as holocausts or 'whole-offerings'. Their blood was sprinkled to purge the sanctuary, but the rest of the animals' bodies was burnt outside the camp (v. 27, see comment on the next verse). In other words, the animals were not used, as in some other sacrifices, in sacred meals. The writer of Hebrews reinterprets this fact to show the limited rights enjoyed by Old Testament priests. Christians, by contrast, share in the sacrifice in which Christ's blood, not that of an animal, was shed or sprinkled for their purification.

Readers of Hebrews continue to disagree, as they have done for centuries, about whether or not this verse refers to the Lord's Supper. On the whole, Roman Catholics have tended to think that it does, while Protestants have tended to interpret it as referring to the sacrifice of Christ on the cross. There are, however, important exceptions on both sides. The Roman Catholic NJB, for example, has a note on the word 'altar' in this verse which reads as follows:

> Not the table used for the Eucharist, but either the cross on which Christ was sacrificed, or Christ himself through whom we offer the sacrifice of prayer to God. Non-Christian Jews who still 'serve the tabernacle' cannot participate.

A study Bible published by the German Bible Society comments:

> Some interpreters see here a reference to the Lord's Supper, but the verse is rather to be understood figuratively: the altar is the cross from which believers live ('eat').

It is difficult, however, to believe that the word 'eat' is entirely figurative, especially since 'food' was mentioned in the previous verse. It is not used in this way anywhere else in the New Testament, except occasionally of fire (Heb. 10.27) or rust (James 5.3) 'eating' in the sense of destroying. It may be that the writer of Hebrews did not wish to risk bringing trouble on his readers by speaking openly about their celebrations of the Lord's Supper. It is not necessary, however, to identify the 'altar' as the table on which the Lord's Supper was celebrated, or to think of the Lord's Supper as an end in itself. The writer's point is that the old and new orders are separate and incommensurable, so that anyone who continues to rely on the ceremonies of the old order prevents himself from sharing in the benefits of Christ's sacrifice, of which v. 12 will speak once more.

13.11   To begin at the end of this verse, the key phrase 'outside the camp' usually refers in Old Testament laws to the Israelite camp during the long march from Egypt to the promised land. In the form in which we now have these laws, however, they often reflect the settled conditions which followed occupation of the land of Israel, and *outside the camp* comes to mean 'outside the Temple area'. The normal practice was for sacrificial animals to be killed, and some of their blood sprinkled at the entrance to the sanctuary or Tent of Meeting (Ex. 29.11; Lev. 4.4; 7.14; 9.8; 16.18f.). Those parts of the animal not used in sacrifice are burnt *outside the camp* (Ex. 29.14; Lev. 4.11f.; 7.17; 9.11; 16.27). There are certain exceptions to this norm. Ex. 33.7 reflects on older tradition in which the Tent of Meeting was itself *outside the camp*. Num. 19.2–10 regulates the sacrifice of a red cow or heifer which is killed 'outside the camp' (v. 3), and whose ashes are also 'deposited . . . outside the camp' (v. 10). This is the ·ritual to which Heb. 9.12 refers. The area *outside the camp* was also a place where ritually unclean groups (Lev. 13.46; Num. 5.3f.) and objects (Lev. 14.40f.) were placed, where the army purified itself (Num. 31.13–20), and where people were punished (Num. 12.14f; 15.35f.).

In the present passage the writer of Hebrews probably does not distinguish between the details of these various accounts. What he does do (as in a different way in 3.1–6) is to reinterpret them in such a way as to turn them almost literally inside out in order to take account of the new fact of Christ. What mattered most for the Old Testament writers was what happened in and around the sanctuary; what happened outside the camp was usually secondary. The writer of Hebrews does not question this as far as the old order is concerned. But the new order is completely different. Jesus' death outside the walls of Jerusalem is reflected in the *stigma* (v. 13) now borne by Christians, especially Jewish Christians (the majority of the first readers of Hebrews) who are 'outside the pale' as far as other Jews are concerned. Christians do not fit into the earthly established order; but they have a permanently established home elsewhere (v. 14).

13.12   For a moment, contrast between the old and new orders gives place to an implied comparison. The instructions for the Day of Atonement liturgy specified that 'Aaron' (and by implication, his successors as high priests) must sprinkle the blood of a bull and a goat 'to make expiation for himself, his household, and the whole assembly of Israel' (Lev. 16.18). The animals were then, as already noted, *taken outside the camp and destroyed by fire* (v. 27). The readers of Hebrews by now need only the gentlest reminder that Jesus offered *his own blood* (9.12), not the blood of animals but *himself* (v. 14); and that he did not, like the levitical high priests, need to offer sacrifice for his own sins (vv. 7.14). Just as the purpose of the Day of Atonement liturgy was to purify or *consecrate the people*, so that is also the purpose of Christ's more effective sacrifice.

But the main point is now the disgrace or *stigma* (v. 13) which Jesus incurred by his death 'outside the gate' of Jerusalem (Mark 15.20ff. and parallels; John 19.17; compare Rev. 14.20). The writer of Hebrews may also be thinking of Deut. 21.18–23, which speaks first of a trial 'at the town gate' (v. 19), and then of a hanging which makes the condemned person 'accursed in the sight of God' (v. 23, which Paul in Gal. 3.13 applies to the crucifixion of Jesus).

13.13   The writer returns to the Old Testament phrase *outside the camp*. The readers cannot now literally join Jesus at Golgotha. What they have to do is identify themselves with him in his earthly humiliation. Like Moses, they are to share *the stigma that rests on God's Anointed* (Heb. 11.26). The writer is probably thinking mainly of Christian Jews being treated by non-Christian Jews as renegades. Faithfulness to Christ means giving up any kind of status in Jewish society, since that society as a whole has not accepted Christ. But there may also be the thought that although Jews were recognized and tolerated in the Roman Empire as a special religious group, that privilege would go, as soon as Roman administrators learned from non-Christian Jews that Christians were different. As early as about 112 CE we have correspondence between Pliny, Governor of Bithynia, and the Emperor Trajan, recognizing Christians as a distinct group.

In any case, the *stigma* which Christians had to bear was real. Paul speaks of apostles being treated 'as the scum of the earth, as the dregs of humanity' (I Cor. 4.13), and of counting his own high status in Judaism as 'so much rubbish, for the sake of gaining Christ' (Phil. 3.8). Some religious groups today, including Orthodox Jews and strict Muslims, are equally harsh to those who leave their ranks in order to become Christians. Other Christians may have to bear more subtle forms of discrimination or loss of status.

13.14   Nevertheless, just as for Jesus the humiliation was only *for a short while* (Heb. 2.9), and he could see in advance *the joy that lay ahead for him* (12.2), so the present humiliation of Christians is greatly outweighed by the permanent home which God has promised them. Again, the writer is reminding his readers of what he has stated more fully before (11.10,16; 12.22).

13.15f.   Verse 10 contrasted the Christian 'altar' with Old Testament worship. Now the writer says a little more of the content of Christian worship, though not about its forms, not even about the Lord's Supper. Nor is there any separation between worship and practical Christian living: both *praise* (v. 15) and *kindness* and sharing (v. 16) are described as *sacrifice*. (Most translations, unlike REB, do not start a new paragraph with v. 16.)

Tribute in v. 15 is literally 'fruit' (RSV, NIV, NJB); REB uses a different metaphor to give the same meaning. The idea of praise of God as a spiritual sacrifice is found already in the Greek Old Testament. The Hebrew text of Hos. 14.2 has: 'we shall pay our vows with cattle from our pens'; but this becomes in the corresponding Greek (v. 3); 'we will repay with the fruit of our lips'. Compare the Hebrew text of Isa. 57.18f., which is translated:

> . . . on the lips of those who mourn [Israel]
> I shall create words of praise.

Psalms of Solomon (first century BCE) 15.3 also speaks in language similar to Hebrews of

> A new psalm with song with a happy heart,
> the fruit of the lips with the tuned instrument of the tongue,
> the first fruits of the lips from a devout and righteous heart.

To *acknowledge* (literally, 'confess', GNB, NIV, as in 11.13) *his* (God's) *name* means to maintain *the faith we profess* as Christians (3.1; 4.14; compare 10.23). This in turn probably entails both inner faithfulness and outward witness.

In v. 16 *never neglect* is the same as 'do not neglect' in v. 2; *never* is not in the text. Both verses speak of practical help. To show *kindness* is literally 'well-doing'; the kinds of actions mentioned in 10.33f. and 13.2f. *To share what you have with others* translates a single word, *koinonia*, which may refer either to material or spiritual sharing. In

Acts 2.42 it is translated 'to share the common life', but it may refer there to the sharing of property between Christians. In Rom. 15.26 the same word is translated 'a fund'. In the present verse the writer is probably thinking mainly of material help to fellow-Christians in special need, but wider forms of sharing are not excluded. Even such material contributions are *sacrifices* which God will honour.

In 13.17 the writer returns to the leaders of the Christian community, first mentioned in v. 7. He tells us nothing of how these leaders were chosen. His silence on this and related matters may suggest that the first leaders, and perhaps even their successors, were appointed in some less formal manner than that described in the Pastoral Epistles, where Paul is represented as commissioning Timothy and Titus, and instructing them to appoint others. The writer of Hebrews draws no parallel with the appointment of Jewish high priests, or with the appointment of Jesus as high priest (5.1–10). Nothing can be proved from the silence of one letter, but there is much evidence that the problem of visible authority in local churches soon arose (see I Cor. 1.10–17; 16.16). The purpose of I Clement, written about 96 CE, also to Corinth, and influenced by Hebrews, is written to uphold the authority of 'bishops and deacons' (42.4) appointed by the apostles. Ignatius, writing at the beginning of the second century CE, was already instructing his readers to be 'obedient to the bishop as to Jesus Christ' (*Trallians* 2.1). Authority in the church continues to be a problem, both between different denominations and within local churches. Hebrews recognizes the beginnings of the problem without prescribing a particular answer.

Several motives are given for obedience to the leaders. First, the leaders, literally, 'are keeping watch over your souls' (RSV). Secondly, closely linked with the first point, their authority is balanced by responsibility to God at the last day (similar language is used in Matt. 12.36; I Peter 4.5, but of Pharisees and pagans respectively). Third, it is the ordinary members' responsibility to make sure that the leaders' *work brings them happiness, not pain and grief*. Fourth, to do otherwise *would be no advantage* to the members of the community. This heaping up of motives may suggest something of the anxiety of Paul in I Cor. 14.33–40, accumulating reasons why women should not speak in public worship; but the tone in Hebrews is quieter and less polemical.

13.18f. *We* in v. 18 probably refers to a real group of evangelists including the author; v. 19, by contrast, refers to the author alone (*I*) for the first time, except in passing in 11.32. The contrast is brought out by the word *specially*, implicit in the text. The writer, unlike Paul, does not spend much time defending himself to his readers; but like Paul (Rom. 15.30ff.; Eph. 6.19f.; II Thess. 3.1f.), he asks for the support of their prayer.

We do not know whether the writer was prevented by imprisonment, or for some other reason, from visiting his readers and speaking with them personally. Whatever the obstacle was, it is no doubt the reason for his writing, so we may be grateful.

Always in v. 18 is literally 'in everything' (NJB); less probably 'among everyone'.

13.20–25   *Conclusion*

13.20f.   The writer's blessing of his readers is eloquent. It contains some traditional language, including the only direct reference in Hebrews to the resurrection of Jesus. There is however no reason to suppose that the writer did not compose it himself, since it includes a reference to the central theme of the epistle, the new covenant sealed by Christ's sacrificial death. The first part of v. 20 recalls Isa. 63.11, which speaks of God as

> he who brought up from the Nile
> the shepherd of his flock,

that is, in the Old Testament setting, Moses. The last words of v. 20 may mean either (1) 'by' (RSV, NJB) or *through* (REB, NIV), or (2) 'with' (AV), that is, accompanied by, *the blood of an eternal covenant*. Of the two alternatives, (1) is to be preferred, but neither is entirely clear. Perhaps the best solution is GNB's restructuring of this part of the sentence. 'God has raised from death our Lord Jesus, who is the Great Shepherd of the sheep as the result of his sacrificial death, by which the eternal covenant is sealed.' The theme of God as his people's shepherd runs right through the Old Testament and into the New; see for example Ps. 23; Ezek. 34.11–16; Matt. 2.6 (applying Micah 5.1 to Jesus); Mark 14.27, echoing Zech. 13.7; John 10, especially vv. 11,14; and especially I Peter 5.4, of Jesus as 'chief shepherd'.

From him (v. 21), *all goodness* may be expected and hoped for. Some manuscripts have 'every good action' (compare NJB). Instead of *create in us*, some manuscripts have '. . . in you' (RSV text, GNB). Some manuscripts omit 'and ever'. Such variations are common near the end of books.

13.22   *I beg* is the same as 'I ask' in v. 19; the corresponding noun is translated appeal, literally, 'word of appeal', 'exhortation' (RSV, NIV), 'strengthening' or 'encouragement'. The same range of meaning is found in the related word translated 'advocate' in John 14.26 and elsewhere, speaking of the Holy Spirit. In the present verse, GNB translates 'message of encouragement', and this is probably the main effect which the writer hoped his letter would have. His appeals and warnings are in the end related to that positive purpose.

The phrase *a short letter* has been taken as evidence that ch. 13 circulated apart from the rest of the letter; but this is unlikely. The author probably means that he has written relatively briefly for such a great subject, or such a serious situation. Similar language is used in I Peter 5.12.

13.23   Most translations understand the beginning of this verse to mean that the writer is giving his readers news about Timothy; less probably, it may mean, 'as you know.' *Our friend* is literally 'our brother', as Paul calls Timothy in I Thess. 3.2.

Most translations take the next part of the verse to mean that Timothy has been released from prison, and this is probably correct, though the word may merely mean that he had gone away. Nothing else is known of this imprisonment of Timothy. The travel details mentioned towards the end of the verse were no doubt clear to the readers, but we cannot reconstruct them with certainty.

13.24   The first part of this verse suggests once more (as in vv. 7,17) that the intended readers are not the leaders of the Christian community, and also suggests for the first time that they are not the entire membership of their church. This may imply that they are one of several house churches in a large town or city such as Rome, or less probably Corinth. *All God's people* is literally, 'all the saints' (RSV); as always in the New Testament, they are seen, not as individuals, but as 'God's holy people' (NJB) as a group.

The second half of the verse may imply either (1) that the writer is with friends in Italy who join him in sending greetings to the readers; or (2) that a group of Italians living somewhere outside Italy join the writer in sending greetings, perhaps back to fellow-Christians in their home country. (2) may be more likely, as in RSV's 'those who come from Italy', but we cannot be sure, so REB translates ambiguously *our Italian friends*.

13.25   The writer's last word is about *God's grace; God's* is implied. This is not an original message, but it is a recurring note in Hebrews (see comment on 2.9; also 13.9 and elsewhere). In the end, for the readers, as in the beginning for Christ (see comment on 1.2,4), everything is a gift from God.